The Bad Detective

Contents

THE BAD DETECTIVE

BOB GORDON

Acknowledgements

It is a pleasure to acknowledge the contributions of many people to this book. At Dundas District High School Jim Regan ignited my fascination with history and at McMaster University Dr John Weaver introduced me to the rigours of the discipline. My interest in Detective Power was initiated by Debra Komar and fostered by Trevor Adams, editor of *Halifax Magazine*. At the Halifax Municipal Archives Susan McClure and her assistant, Elena Cremonese, repeatedly went above and beyond to assist. Marlene Miller, *ex-officio* archivist of the Halifax Regional Police provided the photograph of the department proudly assembled in front of the new, in 1892, city hall. The staff of the Local History Room at the Halifax Central Library also frequently offered up unexpected gems. Donna Pym, at the costume department of the Royal Ontario Museum in Toronto, provided valuable background on fashion and attire in the late-Victorian era.

Invaluable technical support was provided by Darryl and Jim. Glenys Causton read drafts and was supportive throughout. Finally, but foremost, I am more grateful than words can express to my brother, David, for everything from editorial assistance to hospitality and all points in between.

Published in Great Britain in 2021
by Banovallum Books
an imprint of Mortons Books Ltd.
Media Centre
Morton Way
Horncastle, LN9 6JR

BANOVALLUM BOOKS

ISBN 978 1 911658 36 8

The right of Bob Gordon to be identified as the author of this work has been asserted in accordance with the Copyright, Designs and Patents Act 1988.
Typeset by Jayne Clements, Hinoki Design and Typesetting (jayne@hinoki.co.uk)
Printed and bound by Gutenburg, Malta

Foreword

Let me tell you the secret that has led me to my goal.
My strength lies solely in my tenacity.
LOUIS PASTEUR—CHEMIST, BACTERIOLOGIST

THIS IS the story of a police officer whose time in the Halifax Police Department ended over a century ago. Nicholas Power joined the department in the colony of Nova Scotia only weeks after its establishment in 1864, three years before the Dominion of Canada came into existence. When he retired as Chief of Police in 1907, 40 years after Confederation, he had spent almost a quarter of a century as the department's sole detective. He was, in fact, the only official, full-time police department detective in the Maritimes, and one of only a handful in Canada in the late-Victorian era.

He also was frequently unscrupulous and shameless, yet deported a reputation for minute observation, faultless ratiocination and unfailing intuition.

Power's was a world of horses, carriages and steam locomotives before the automobile. The few streets were gas-lit and country lanes were truly dark as night. The burgeoning railroad network and the telegraph were radical innovative technologies. Electrification was a new-fangled sensation not entirely to be trusted, as were canoodling and wheeling. Forensic science was but a primitive art and often dismissed by jurors accustomed to plain old common sense. In many ways this bygone era is a foreign land. However, the story of this bad detective is distressingly familiar in many respects.

Detective Power's singularity resulted in his involvement in virtually all major crimes in the region, and often found him investigating and, subsequently, testifying in cases far afield, including the US. The result was a growing public profile, as newspapers increasingly documented his achievements. It culminated in comparisons to Sherlock Holmes, at the time wildly popular, and that is what makes this a jarringly contemporary story. With growing literacy and cheaper newspapers, the press was the social media of the day and Power knew how to use it. Such was his skill that many tales of derring-do easily disprovable became part of his myth. In large measure he was a social media creation in an era when crime filled the front pages and newspapers released specials many times a day during the most sensational trials. In terms of manipulating 'social' media, Power's machinations are shockingly modern. The basis of his fame, the foundation myth that his reputation has rested on into the 21st century, is exactly that, a myth. A myth of his own making amplified by yellow journalism. Power's public persona as a master of detection was not founded on fact, it was a creation of Power's, with a willing popular press broadcasting his message.

'Fake news' is not new news. Rumours, complete fabrications, 'fake', even multiple and contradictory reports, were *de rigueur* on a slow news day in the late-Victorian age. Canadian newspapers were far more willing to print 'fake news' than anything media outlets are even accused of today. And, on the other side of the fence, Detective Power was willing to twist his answers and grant his interviews in order to try a case in the court of public opinion long before the legal system ruled. Frequently, this is an uncomfortably contemporary tale of 'fake' news. Power needed the newspapers to disseminate his narratives, and the newshounds needed Power to fill column inches. It was a mutually beneficial relationship with both sides lying freely when it suited their purposes. Both occupations were less constrained by ethical norms and legal restraints than they are today, so 'fake news' of all sorts abounded. Again, a painfully modern problem.

This is a thoroughly modern tale also in that it involves terrorism. Terrorism, politically motivated violence committed by non-state actors directed against the wider society rather than strictly military targets characterises the modern era: airports and train stations are targeted, civilian airliners are shot down and innocent children are killed and maimed. A terrorist attack employing an improvised explosive device, yes, an IED as in Iraq and Afghanistan, is the subject of the first chapter. A Fenian attack on the royal family with a homemade bomb is terrorism. The employment of an IED to kill a public figure, regardless of collateral civilian damage, could be current. Fear of terrorism was as real to the reading public in the 1880s as it is today. New technologies had frighteningly increased terrorists' capacity to wreak havoc. There were plots and plots foiled, rumours and, all too often, successful bombings and assassinations. The 'War on Terror' is old news. It is a key component of bad Detective Power's policing, at the heart of his foundation myth, and suggestive of his *modus operandi* throughout his career.

Finally, this is often a story of official malfeasance, frequently with an undercurrent of racism, an issue hardly unknown today. Whether malevolent or merely ignorant will be for the reader to decide. Notably, this remains a persistent question in Power's hometown, known today as the Halifax Regional Municipality (HRM). Concerns have been raised about random street checks, colloquially known as 'carding', and their preponderant impact on minorities. Cornwallis Park, opposite the recently restored Canadian Pacific railroad station was recently denuded of its eponymous central statue as Mi'kmaq (indigenous) groups protested the commemoration of Halifax's founder, a man who offered a bounty for Mi'kmaq scalps. Social media, 'fake' news, terrorism and police/minority relations are all key themes throughout Power's policing career. Thoroughly modern in every way.

When Detective Nicholas Power died in his 90s the hagiography silently slid over the fact that he was a bad detective. His frequent wrongful convictions, convictions overturned on appeal and diverse other errors and failures testify to a bad, as in unskilled, investigator. More importantly, morally he was a bad man. His actions had evil consequences. He destroyed the lives of innocent people, allowing the guilty to run free and heinous crimes to go unpunished. Nicholas Power was never Canada's Sherlock Holmes, he was just a bad detective who knew how to shine his media image as well as his badge and buttons. But pity those who paid the price when his predatory gaze settled on them, because Detective Nicholas Power was nothing if he was not tenacious.

CHAPTER ONE

Saving the Prince, the Future King George V

"ANOTHER DYNAMITE SCARE!" *The Morning Herald* headline screamed in caps. Reassuringly, the lead added, "Two Suspicious Characters Arrested." In October 1883 His Royal Highness Prince George (Frederick Ernest Albert) of Wales, future King George V, was visiting Halifax while serving in the Royal Navy aboard HMS *Canada*. The *Herald* story reported Halifax Police Department's newly minted detective, Nicholas Power, had prevented a terrorist attempt to blow up the *Canada* and kill the Prince. Power's astute detective work had prevented the murder of the future king. Thirty years later Power would be rewarded for his diligence with the King's Police Medal. Fifty years later the accolades persisted, in 1934 a glowing feature in *The Halifax Mail* included an interview titled 'Tells Of Part In Preventing Murder Of Britain's King'. Four years later his obituaries repeated and reinforced the tale. Saving the Prince made Detective Nicholas Power's career.

In the 1880s Englishmen felt Albion was erupting beneath their feet. As is the case today, the press, public, police and politicians were all consumed by a relentless, seemingly endless and apparently unstoppable terrorist bombing campaign. Stabbings, shootings, assassinations and other acts of terrorism were also on the bill of fare. The incident Power prevented was only one of many throughout the Empire. Ireland was enraged and determined a price must be paid by the English and their empire.

Failed efforts at land reform in the 1870s gave rise to an increasingly radical nationalist opposition to English rule in Ireland. Charles Parnell's Land League advocating passive, non-violent obstruction was out-paced by the Irish Republican Brotherhood. A violent splinter group from the Brotherhood, the Irish National 'Invincibles' advocated aggression. They wanted to bomb England, Scotland and Wales. They wanted to take the fight to the enemy using the only means available, homemade bombs—in very contemporary terms IEDs, improvised explosive devices. They were terrorists and they were successful. They terrorised the population in the home islands and the colonies, particularly the largest

Royal Navy port in the northwestern Atlantic, Detective Power's Halifax. Nic Power was an Irish Roman Catholic, as was his boss Marshall Garrett Cotter, but he was no Republican. He had proudly served in Her Majesty's Royal Navy and he was determined to do his job and detect terrorists before they had a chance to strike. The Fenians, the North American counterparts of the Brotherhood, were the target of Power's investigations.

In England the terror campaign opened in January 1881. The Invincibles bombed Salford Barracks in Manchester, killing a child. Four months later, and 40 miles west, it was the barracks at Chester. After nine days, on May 16, the police station in Liverpool was targeted and on June 10, 1881 the city hall suffered the same fate. Four bombings in six months. This campaign dominated the news cycle in the same way that terrorism does today. A hysterical public saw a fire-eyed bomber under every bed.

Amid this string of bombings, on Sunday, March 13, 1881, Tsar Alexander II of Russia was assassinated. Explosive-throwing anarchists caught him as he travelled into the *Mikhailovsky Manezh* riding academy in central St Petersburg to review the military roll call. One year later, in March 1882, a pistol-wielding assassin was foiled in an attempt on the life of Queen Victoria. Mentally ill, Roderick Maclean had no connection to Irish issues but this eighth, and final, attempt on the Queen's life only increased the sense of a society at risk. From every side, for a vast array of reasons, maniacs and extremists of every stripe seemed to threaten social stability and cultural touchstones.

Back in Dublin, in May 1882, the Phoenix Park murders had everything to do with the Irish conflict. Liberal British Prime Minister William Ewart Gladstone had to deal with the resignation of his hardline, Quaker, chief secretary of Ireland, William Edward Forster, Liberal MP for Bradford. He replaced him with Lord Frederick Cavendish. Cavendish was a protégé of the Prime Minister, with extensive experience in Parliament. He took the oath as chief secretary at Dublin Castle, on the morning of Saturday, May 6, 1882.

His residence was in Phoenix Park (currently known as Deerfield, it is the residence of the US Ambassador to Ireland). It was adjacent to the vice-regal lodge, now the official residence, Áras an Uachtaráin, and principal workplace of the President of Ireland. Thomas Henry Burke, the permanent under-secretary, also had a residence in the Park. As Cavendish and Burke strolled arm-in-arm through the bucolic lanes of the Park later that day, knife-wielding Invincibles, Joe Brady and Tim Kelly, murdered them both. The unlucky Cavendish had survived less than 12 hours in his new office. Along with Brady and Kelly, Michael Fagan, Thomas Caffrey and Dan Curley were convicted of the murder and were hanged by William Marwood in Kilmainham Gaol in Dublin between May 14 and June 9, 1883. Surprisingly, Brady's name will turn up again in Power's story.

A panicked government passed the Prevention of Crime Act but the bombings continued, targeting Glasgow on January 20, 1883. Two months later London was rocked by a coordinated series of bombings. The targets on March 15 included *The Times*, the Local Government Board and other government buildings on Parliament Street. Police raids in Ireland were uncovering caches of rifles, ammunition, and large stores of dynamite. It seemed as if there were Invincibles with bombs everywhere.

The newly invented explosive dynamite increased the lethality of their blasts exponentially. Previously nitroglycerin had been available but it was notoriously unstable, banned in many jurisdictions and responsible for an accidental explosion in a Wells Fargo office in California that killed 15 people in 1866. The next year, 1867, Alfred Nobel discovered how to stabilise nitroglycerin by adding diatomaceous earth. Ironically, Nobel, of Peace Prize fame, made an instant, explosive impact. Prior to the invention of dynamite, black powder was the most practicable explosive to be had. For a host of reasons, it was impossible to create a compact and portable bomb using black powder. The kegs of powder required to generate a significant blast were impossible to conceal.

There is, of course, the exception that proves the rule. In 1605 an attempt to assassinate King James I by blowing up the entire House of Lords during the State Opening of Parliament on November 5 was betrayed.

On November 4, Guy Fawkes was discovered guarding 36 barrels of gunpowder in the undercroft of the House of Lords. Had the plot succeeded the Lords would have been obliterated: The King and the entire English aristocratic, ruling class eliminated. The Gunpowder Plot by its very name—it is *the* Gunpowder Plot, not *a* Gunpowder Plot—demonstrates bombing in the age of black powder was possible, but it was exceedingly difficult and very rare. Guy Fawkes Day continues to be celebrated in England with fireworks, bonfires and burning effigies of the bomber, and 'anonymous' protesters favour his moustachioed masks.

Dynamite changed the rules of the game. Suddenly, a single stick, about the size of a candle, weighing seven ounces, could destroy a small building. Imagine what a dozen sticks, easily concealed in a small satchel, portmanteau or box could do! It is no exaggeration to state that this revolutionary development transformed terrorist activity as much as nuclear weapons revolutionised 20th century warfare. Dynamite had an equally significant impact on everything from mining and railway construction to warfare. In Detective Power's Halifax, F D Corbett & Co, at 135 Lower Water Street, proudly advertised that it was the sole agent of Nobel's Explosive Company and targeted its advertising at miners.

The seemingly endless, steady stream of bombings was tearing at the edge of public attitudes. The hysterical newspaper coverage—crime sells and 'if it bleeds it leads'—was as true then as it is today, and it increased pressure on the government for a response. The first attempt, changes at the top in Ireland, had cost Lord Cavendish, Burke and five of the assassins their lives. Next, the Criminal Investigation Division (widely known after the location of its headquarters as Scotland Yard) decided that the creation of an Irish Branch dedicated to combatting nationalist terrorism was necessary. On March 20, 1883 Liberal Home Secretary William Vernon Harcourt authorised a 12-man force to focus on Irish nationalist violence, to be known as the Irish Branch or Irish Brigade.

One year later, in a stunning attack, a bomb was placed in a public urinal in Scotland Yard directly beneath the Irish Branch. The offices were vacant at the time, there were no fatalities, but documents and records were destroyed. The sophistication, daring and creativity of the attack was obvious, and the humiliation of Scotland Yard could not have been more complete. The detectives of the Irish Branch had egg on their faces in their own kitchen.

Across the pond, in the newly unified colonies of British North America, known as the Dominion of Canada since Confederation in 1867, this news of terrorism and IEDs was received with concern. The Fenian Brotherhood was the North American face of Irish nationalism and animosity towards Fenians ran deep in the new Dominion. In Ottawa, less than one year after Confederation, in April 1868 the Irish-Canadian politician

Thomas D'Arcy McGee was felled by a Fenian bullet as he returned to his Ottawa boarding house after a late debate in Parliament. His assassin, Patrick J Whelan, would be the last man to be publicly hanged in Canada.

The site of his execution, the Nicholas Street Gaol, constructed in 1862 and currently a Hostelling International hostel, offers an interesting variation on the architecture of the scaffold and noose. Visitors today can tour the facility and its unique arrangements for providing spectators with the best sight lines. The death chamber is located on the top floor of the facility. It is cantilevered off the side of the building and the trap door beneath the scaffold is located in the floor. The prisoner was 'dropped' by opening the trap door, exposing the dangling prisoner to the crowd assembled below. Subsequently, various methods were devised to shift executions *in camera*. They were moved inside prison walls, even indoors, or an elevated scaffold was replaced with a noose at grade, with the condemned man being dropped into an excavated pit. Haligonians remembered the last man publicly hanged in Canada was a Fenian assassin.

The Fenian Brotherhood, founded in the US in 1858 by John O'Mahony, a former colonel of the 69th Regiment of New York State Militia, and Michael Doheny, was the American affiliate of the Irish Republican Brotherhood. In the wake of the US Civil War many Fenians had Civil War combat experience like their leader. They also shared a bizarre world view. The Brotherhood would attain Ireland's independence by invading the British colonies in North America. Having occupied them they would then trade the colonies back to Britain in exchange for Irish independence. It was a geopolitical exchange of hostage territory. Quixotic as the dream may have been, that was their story and they were sticking to it. And they were ready to act on it, five times in fact.

The largest battle was fought on the Niagara peninsula, in present day Ontario, the scene of some of the major battles of the War of 1812 half a century earlier. At Ridgeway, a Fenian invasion force of 700 routed a larger Canadian militia force and drove them from the field on June 2, 1866. They were unable to exploit their victory and, fearing approaching British redcoats, they were forced to retire back across the Niagara River, victorious but frustrated. They had won the battle but lost the war.

It was not Ridgeway that concerned Haligonians the most. Months before Ridgeway, in the spring of 1866, Fenians numbering some 700 had threatened Campobello Island, famous as Franklin D Roosevelt's beloved summer home, in New Brunswick. Sitting astride the entrance of the Bay of Fundy it is less than 50 miles from Nova Scotia's southern tip. Led by O'Mahony the Fenians assembled a small fleet and prepared to mount an amphibious operation against the island. British commander Charles Hastings Doyle, stationed at Halifax, responded with 'shock and awe'. He dispatched a naval squadron transporting Royal Marines and

British regulars immediately. Choosing discretion over valour, O'Mahony's forces melted away, reappearing months later at Ridgeway. While the invasion had been pre-empted, the wariness lingered. Memories of the Fenian menace were real and recent in Halifax in 1883.

The Fenian threat was as present to Canadians as the bombing campaign in England and Scotland was to its victims. According to Canadian historian Desmond Morton: "For another couple of generations, Fenians became the handiest bogey for any politician faced with unrest or disaffection." Since Confederation in 1867, Gilbert McMicken a small town, small time businessman, minor functionary and political hack, had been Sir John A Macdonald's erstwhile spymaster, detailed specifically to penetrate Fenian organisations and betray planned operations against Canada. So desperate was the fear of Fenians that early in his career McMicken had proposed to Macdonald, "one or two clever women whose absolute virtue stands questioned by the censorious" to get "susceptible members of the 'senate' [the Fenian leadership] into their toils and thus, as Delilah with Sampson, possess themselves of their secrets." Fear of Fenians haunted the hallowed halls of government and reached down into the labourers' saloons.

The perception of a Fenian threat endured in the memories of Haligonians with astonishing dynamism. Halifax Aldermen Patrick M Duggan, Ward 3, and Andrew Hubley, Ward 4, loathed one another and the two engaged in regular donnybrooks, replete with personal insults, and even a quarter of a century after the Fenian raids they recalled them as yesterday. During a Police Committee meeting in 1893 the animus endured when the latter spat out this ancient insult: "The true secret of your malice against the deputy marshall is this. That at the time of the last Fenian invasion the Fenian flag was flying over your father's house, and the deputy marshall compelled him to take it down. Now, after all these years, you're a small enough man to hound the deputy for what he did then."

The Fenians were also a favourite target of the newspapers across the new Dominion. Moreover, they were entirely willing to link the North American Fenians to the extremists in England and Ireland. On May 6, 1883, *The Morning Herald* reported that a Fenian plot to blow up Queen's Park, the Ontario legislature, had been uncovered. The solidly Tory *Herald* condemned the Ontario Grits for trying to make political hay of the discovery. Two days later, still two months before the Prince arrived, *The Globe* (Toronto) reported Fenian rumours threatening Halifax. It noted that Canadian Prime Minister Sir John A Macdonald sent a letter to Nova Scotia's Lieutenant-Governor Archibald warning, "that two suspicious vessels, manned, it was believed, by Fenians, and carrying a quantity of torpedoes [referred to today as mines] and other dangerous explosives, had sailed from Boston a few days ago, and it was thought intended to make Halifax their destination... with the intention of blowing up shipping entering or leaving." Particularly worrisome was May 14, "the day on which [Joe] Brady, one of the Phoenix Park murderers, is to be executed, it was also recommended that the guards at the various barracks, powder magazines, dockyards, and warships in port should be strengthened." It did not require a prince in port, only an imaginary assault, for Fenian rumours to flare up. The bogey that was the Fenians was as good for the press as it was for the politicians.

In Nic Power's Halifax, the fear of Fenian violence was as real, deep-seated and persistent as it was in London, England in 1883. Haligonians were not unaware of the bombing campaign in England, nor were they tolerant of it. On October 19, on the front page, *The Morning Herald* reprinted a letter to the *Irish Canadian* from former British Member of Parliament A M Sullivan. His conclusion was shockingly straightforward. If the moderate Irish nationalists cannot reign in the bombers, they "will be exterminated by exasperated Englishmen as monsters." Hyperbole, threats and extreme sentiments typified Irish issues in the early 1880s on both sides of the Atlantic. In 1883 everybody in Halifax was up in arms about the Fenians: the politicians, the press, the public and Power. Power was acutely aware of the widely held, popular perception that Fenians were a real and present danger. He was determined that nothing would happen on his watch.

Fear and loathing of Fenians was alive and well when HMS *Canada*, and its princely cargo, steamed into her berth in the Bedford Basin. The *Canada* had departed Portsmouth on June 13, touched at Plymouth on June 19 and spent the week from June 29 to July 3 at Madeira. Storms from June 23 to June 25 tore off the top gallant mast, but otherwise the trip had been uneventful. It would serve three years on the North America and West Indies Station.

Laid down in 1879 and launched on August 26, 1881, the *Canada* was a *Comus*-class screw corvette. Built in the Portsmouth Royal Dockyard, she was one of the newest additions to the Royal Navy. Powered by a three-cylinder horizontal compound engine with one high-pressure cylinder flanked by two low-pressure cylinders, she had a metal frame and hull, the latter copper-sheathed. The lower deck was used for storage, her 10 BL six-inch Mk II guns were mounted on the quarterdeck, with her boilers and engine amidship. She was barque-rigged with the fore and mainmasts square-rigged and only the mizzen rigged fore-and-aft. The single smokestack protruded between the fore and mainmasts. She was a state-of-the-art ship, as quick and deadly as she appeared; an appropriate appointment for a royal middie.

Interestingly, three of her crew remain in Canada to this day. They are interred in the Royal Naval Burying Ground, now on the grounds of the Naval Museum of

Halifax. It is also the oldest military cemetery in Canada. While only 89 stone markers remain, it is estimated that approximately 400 Royal Navy personnel were interred overall.

The comings and goings of Royal Navy vessels had been a common sight in Halifax for over a century but never passed unremarked. The Royal Navy was, literally, Halifax's *raison d'etre*. Frequently, the arrival of Her Majesty's ships was greeted with receptions, dinners and concerts. And for the *Canada* it was only more so, because the 18-year-old Prince was among the ship's complement. In the early evening of August 1, she sailed through The Narrows into Bedford Basin and settled in a berth. The Prince, accompanied by the captain of the *Canada*, Frances Durrant, came ashore and the pair were feted with a concert in Halifax's beautiful public gardens.

Prince George was a true sailor. Being only third in line to the throne, behind his father and elder brother, he was permitted a full-time naval career. In 1883 the Prince was a midshipman, or 'middie'. Essentially an apprentice officer, middies lived in a sort of limbo, between the privileges of the officers and the privations of the lower decks. *The Globe* (Toronto) described the Prince as "a slender youth, in height one or two inches over five feet, with light-coloured hair and a fair complexion." *The Transcript* (Boston) offered a more intimate portrait: "He has a rounder face than his elder brother, [Prince Albert Victor (Christian Edward), Duke of Clarence and Avondale] full lips that easily curve into smiles and a very pleasant expression." The Halifax *Herald* relayed a superior officer's glowing report: "Yes we like the Prince well... He is pretty lively and enjoys a lark as well as any of us." However, with the death of his older brother during an influenza pandemic in 1892, he became the Heir Presumptive after his father and was required to resign from the Royal Navy. The death of Prince Albert may have been a blessing in disguise for the English monarchy, as 'Bertie' was widely regarded as a witless dunderhead. The Prince, ruling as George V, undistinguished but steadfast, would see England through a constitutional crisis in 1910, World War One including the Easter Uprising in Ireland and the Great Depression of the 1930s. His survival, fulfilling his as yet unseen destiny to ascend the throne would have been pre-empted had Fenian bombers succeeded in assassinating him in 1883.

Following a brief, uneventful stay in Halifax, the Prince undertook a tour of the new Dominion of Canada. Accompanied by the flagship of the North America and West Indies Station, HMS *Dido*, a wooden, Eclipse-class screw corvette launched in 1869, and HMS *Northampton*, a Nelson-class armoured cruiser, HMS *Canada*, with the Prince and his party, including his older sister, Princess Louise (Caroline Alberta), Duchess of Argyll aboard, sailed for Quebec City.

After touring Quebec City, they boarded a special

train destined for the capital, Ottawa. The Prince visited William James Topley's studio on Sparks Street, sitting for a portrait. Photography was another new technology and portraits were all the rage. Topley's in Ottawa, Notman's Studio on Bleury Street in Montreal with branches in other cities including Halifax and Climo's on Barrington Street in Halifax were the leading photographers in Canada at the time. In Ottawa the Prince then visited Parliament Hill and toured the neo-Gothic Centre Block with its stunning croft chapter house library. The library was appended to the Centre Block and isolated with steel fire doors to protect the main structure if a fire erupted among the library's highly flammable contents. Ironically, when careless smoking caused a fire that destroyed the Centre Block in 1916, the fire doors protected the library and it alone survived the fire. Presently, and for the next decade, the Centre Block is closed, undergoing extensive renovations and additions.

The Prince also visited the Geological Museum on Sussex Drive, formerly the Clarendon Hotel. His party then went down to the Ottawa River, across the LeBreton Flats to the Chaudière Falls where the Prince inspected James McLaren's mills and sash factory. McLaren was a wealthy, local entrepreneur close to the Prime Minister, Sir John A Macdonald. He employed almost 100 men and produced lumber and mouldings valued at about $200,000 annually.

The party's special train steamed overnight towards

Toronto and all points west, which at the time meant southwestern Ontario. It would not be until 1905 that Saskatchewan and Alberta would join the Confederation and Canada would extend continuously from the Pacific Coast to the Atlantic Coast. In Toronto they stayed at the Queen's Hotel, officially as guests of Lord Lorne, Canada's youngest and first royal Governor-General. The Prince visited the Toronto Industrial Exhibition—a forward-looking misnomer as the fair featured livestock and farm implements in all but one of the 23 wooden buildings—the Crystal Palace—devoted to agriculture. In 1882 the fairgrounds became the first site in the city to be lit by electricity. The vice-regal visitor was also amazed by the electric railway Torontonian J J Wright unveiled there that year. The Prince spent the remainder of the day sailing and visiting the Royal Canadian Yacht Club.

Foregoing the Industrial Exhibition, the Princess toured the Hospital for Sick Children and the House of Providence before returning to the Queen's Hotel. That evening the Philharmonic Society and militia bands presented a musical performance in Queen's Park. Wet weather notwithstanding, *The Globe*'s correspondent was impressed. "Every moment the crowd grew larger as it surged about the open space in front of the platform. Wonderful to say the vast majority were ladies, and the vast majority of these were young ladies. Nearly every one wore a gossamer waterproof with the hood drawn over the head, and as they moved about it seemed as if a new race of amphibious creatures had suddenly peopled the Park." Purple prose indeed, but par for the course for newshounds of that era, for whom hyperbole was merely standard operating procedure.

Early the next morning the royals were off to Cobourg, scheduled to inspect the local militia camp. According to *The Globe*: "On their alighting a royal salute of 21 guns was fired by the batteries on the grounds, while all the town bells rang forth a merry peal of welcome. The Princess expressed her admiration at the fine appearance of the Brigade and the beautiful situation of the camp." Then they were on to Kingston, arriving at the city hall in mid-afternoon for an official civic welcome. They then proceeded to the Royal Military College.

August and September are fair and exhibition season in Canada, a tradition that persists today. Not surprisingly, the royals also visited exhibitions in Hamilton and Niagara (formerly Newark, currently Niagara-on-the-Lake and not to be confused with Niagara Falls, although the Prince did visit the famous cataract). Enthusiastic crowds greeted the vice-regal party throughout the province. Mid-October saw the Prince and his entourage return to Halifax, potentially to their doom, but blithely unaware of the Fenians' plans.

Nicholas Power joined the Halifax Police Department as a constable in 1864 fresh out of the Royal Navy. Approximately a decade later he made sergeant and after another decade, upon the death of Detective William

Hutt, he was promoted to that plainclothes role. He had been a detective almost two years when the Prince returned to Halifax and reverted from visiting royalty to humble middie again. The sophomore investigator, with the recent threat of a Fenian attack on shipping fresh on his mind, was determined that nothing would happen to the Prince on his watch.

Exercising due diligence, Detective Power set out to scan the registers and question the owners of the local hotels and boarding houses. Before the era of civil rights, warrants and legal niceties this was standard operating procedure for detectives. Strolling along the wooden sidewalks of Barrington Street, Power paused at Jacob Street and looked right toward the bird's nest of spars and masts in the harbour below. Power's homburg matched his double-breasted gabardine sack coat. With a $40 allowance for clothing Power could afford the best. Gabardine, invented only a few years earlier, was wool waterproofed with lanolin before weaving, which was more comfortable than the rubberised fabric of the traditional Mackintosh. His shield was on the inside of his breast pocket flap, to be flashed with a flick of the wrist. Aside from his imposing presence, his only weapon was a leather sap. Royal Irish Constabulary issue and a nod to his heritage, it was less than a foot long and almost innocent looking. The brown leather covered a steel spring with a one-inch ball bearing on the end. A second flick of his wrist could crack a skull. Twenty stone and six foot, four inches, he briefly contemplated the mud, liberally dosed with horse manure, before he stepped into it and crossed the intersection.

Appearances and attire mattered to Detective Power, even the details. His wide blue hat band was a nod to his two decades 'wearing the blue' before he earned promotion to detective. His bull neck demanded the broad Prince Albert knot of his tie. His image mattered to Detective Power because he knew it influenced others. More than once his massive bulk had won the day without the need for fisticuffs. In similar fashion, his self-confidence and force of personality could be harnessed to assert his narrative of a crime or overwhelm suspects while giving them the third degree.

Across the mired corner and strung along the east side of Barrington, McMurray and Co had three storefronts offering their wide range of millinery stores and dry goods, everything from underwear to outerwear and everything in between, both custom and ready-made, as well as dry goods and furnishings. With five children at home, Power's wife, Mary Jane, was a regular visitor.

Wedged between their storefronts was the entrance to the Parker House Hotel, 277 Barrington Street. Its proprietor, John Creelman, a 57-year-old Presbyterian, his wife and their five children all resided in the hotel. The Parker House's rooms occupied the upper stories above McMurray & Co's storefronts. Power approached Creelman at the desk and requested the register. Two entries caught his attention, William Breckton and James Holmes. They were American, from Boston, with Irish-sounding, probably Roman Catholic names and potentially Fenians.

Power requested, and was granted, access to their room. Remember this was a pre-warrant age. Appeals to a judge for a search warrant were unnecessary. Accompanied by Creelman, the two men entered a room with three beds squeezed into it. Within, amongst various items, were two leather valises against the wall behind one of the beds. According to Creelman's testimony to the subsequent inquiry, "the detective took the small red valise and lifted it on the bed; it was not locked, only strapped." Power loosened the strap and opened it. Staring at the contents he was speechless, so shocked that he proceeded no further. The valise's contents demanded a higher authority even than Detective Power. Realising the gravity of his find, he set off in search of his superior, City Marshall Garrett Cotter. Suppressing his growing excitement, the detective reported his discovery. The innocently nondescript valise contained dynamite, fuses, an alarm clock and all the components of an 'infernal machine', a bomb of some sort, perhaps even a 'time bomb'.

Power immediately set out to arrest the pair. Holmes was arrested quickly. Breckton was run down in an Upper Water Street tavern. They were incarcerated in the damp, dark and dank cells of the old police station on Spring Garden Road.

With the bombers safely locked up in the police station

cells there was no need to rush. It was not until the next day that Power and Cotter returned to the captives' room. Yesterday's scene was repeated, with Cotter doing the honours. "There were packages of dynamite, some fuse, clothing, a clock, some lead, a saw, hammer, a lump of grease, some copper wire and other articles," he testified. The implications were obvious—the whole was greater than the individual parts. The lethal trio were the dynamite, the fuses and the clock and together they added up to a time bomb. American Fenians with a time bomb, exactly like the explosives that Irish bombers were using in England and Scotland, had travelled to Halifax at the same time as the Prince's party returned to the city. Detective Power put the pieces together and detected a plot to kill the Prince.

There was even more incriminating evidence awaiting discovery. When he searched the pair after their arrest, Power found a ticket for checked baggage with the Windsor and Annapolis Railway. The baggage was being stored at the Intercontinental Railway (ICR) depot on North Street. On Wednesday evening Detective Power walked to the ICR station. From the police station he walked down Spring Garden past St Mary's Cathedral. Construction commenced in 1820 and after substantial, neo-Gothic renovations completed in 1874, it was one of only two Roman Catholic cathedrals in Canada and, at 198 feet above the sidewalk, it sported the largest granite spire in North America. It was Detective Power's parish, and he had married Mary Jane Sheehan within, in the spring of 1864. Facing the cathedral was the Old Burying Ground, Halifax's first cemetery. In 1875 both of his parents had made the short trip across the street from funeral to burial, as had his 11-year-old daughter Alice a year later. Turning left at Barrington Street, Power walked over a mile north, through the heart of Halifax to the ICR station at Barrington and North streets.

Power greeted the baggage-masters, Phelan and Clay. In return for the check, they passed over to him a bundle wrapped in osnaburg and bound with a new shawl strap. Power returned to the station with the package unopened. Cautiously, with Marshall Cotter looking over his shoulder, Power loosened the strap and peeled back the coarse cloth. Jules Verne, the famously popular science fiction writer of the era, could not have imagined the contents. It was, according to *The Herald*, "a complete suit of the best rubber material" known at the time variously as a diving skirt or swimming suit. In terrifying detail, *The Herald* described its operation: "It was of a kind never seen here before and could be put on by any person and filled with air, through long tubes, which are fitted with screw stops to prevent the air from escaping. This renders them buoyant, and a man so clothed with one of these suits might float in the water for hours at a time." The *Herald* could only shudder when it speculated on the implications of this discovery, "the numerous threats that have been made out time and again in regard to the destruction of English shipping, it is just possible that they may have had designs in that direction." Detective Power was more than willing to boldly and explicitly make the connection. These men were Fenians, Fenian bombers intent on destroying the Prince, along with HMS *Canada* and her crew. They were terrorists unbothered by collateral damage in their desire to strike a mortal blow at the royal family. Power rushed to inform the newshounds of his discovery and the Fenian plot filled the front pages and headlines.

An inquiry under the stipendiary magistrate was immediately initiated and incriminating evidence steadily accumulated throughout the inquiry. The pair had visited Halifax weeks earlier, at the very time the Prince had first arrived in the summer. They were reported to be always flush, but only occasionally, if at all, employed. Their landlord testified the valises had been carried to the room, stowed behind the bed and remained there untouched since. An experienced miner, John Grant, testified that the fuses and dynamite in their possession were not commonly used in mining. Finally, they had hired a boat and toured the harbour. This was not an unusual pastime for visitors to the city, but surely evidence that they had been conducting an intelligence gathering reconnaissance in preparation for the dastardly deed.

In the press, *The Morning Herald's* reporter used innuendo with masterly effect after he visited their landlady on their previous visit, Mrs Mehan of 71 Dresden Row.

"'Were they Fenians?' eagerly asked Mrs Mehan and continuing: 'Didn't Dan suspect…' Here she cut short a remark that might have thrown some light on the movements of these men." Helpfully, she added that they had once had a visitor who "looked like an American, but said he was reared here in Canada." A revelation by O'Donnell, the third man to share the room, was interrupted: "'They told me one day—' Here Mr Mehan, who had taken a seat beside ODonnell, nudged him with his knee and shook his head. O'Donnell's countenance thereupon underwent a visible change. He didn't finish what he was going to say." Also, the Mehans' "son had some suspicions of the two men." Their current landlord's testimony, "they said they were going to the gold mines to work," was dismissed as an alibi cleverly concocted by Holmes and Breckton to disguise their evil intent.

The story quickly outgrew Halifax and even the Maritimes. On October 23, *The Globe* (Toronto) included an article headlined "THE FENIAN PLOTTERS" that noted: "The Halifax dynamite carriers were provided with a diving dress." The story went on to detail the events during the magistrate's court hearing the day before. The entire day had been spent examining Detective Power. This was because Power had played an essential role in the initial arrest and had been involved in the subsequent investigation throughout, but also because Power loved the limelight and delighted in taking the stand and blowing his own horn. For a full day Power set his narrative in stone, enumerating the incriminating evidence and outlining his narrative. Power enjoyed the spotlight and whether his audience was a judge and jury or journalists, he could rarely resist a chance to talk about himself. Power outlined his initial hunch, the incriminating bomb-making components in their luggage and the checked baggage containing a 'swimming suit' that confirmed a threat against a naval target. He also testified that the men had, while alone with him, confessed to their deadly plans.

It was an open and shut case. The motive was obvious to one and all—they were dangerous and disgruntled Fenians engaged in an irregular or asymmetric conflict with the imperialistic English. The method was shared by the Invincibles and the Fenians in the New World, the revolutionary explosive, dynamite. The opportunity was presented by the presence of the Prince aboard ship coupled with the bombers' 'inflatable swimming suit'. It was all wrapped around a confession that Power had extracted from the two.

With Breckton and Holmes secure in jail awaiting trial in the new year, Power's legend had been made. His initiative in searching for potential trouble, the thoroughness of his investigation, and his erudition in tracing the course, or potential course, of events had prevented the killing of Queen Victoria's grandson. Most importantly he had interrogated the suspects and obtained vital confessions. Power's investigation and testimony were the key pieces of the Crown's case against the Fenian bombers. His miraculous intervention made headlines across Canada and internationally. Having been promoted from wearing the blue to mufti only 20 months earlier, the legend of Detective Nicholas Power was firmly established. Its foundation was his discovery of a Fenian plot against a member of the English royal family. Eight years later, Sherlock Holmes became a cultural keystone with his appearance in *The Strand*. It was not long after that the newspapers began to refer to Detective Power as 'Canada's Sherlock Holmes'.

Three decades after saving the Prince, in 1912, with the Prince now ruling as George V, Power was awarded the King's Police Medal for "special services to Royalty" in recognition of the central role he played in foiling the Fenian bomb plot and saving the Prince, the *Canada* and her crew. Detective Nicholas Power would forever be known as the 'Man who saved the Prince'. For the quarter-century following this incident his shining reputation would see him involved in almost every serious crime in Nova Scotia. Upon his death he was hailed as Canada's most erudite and widely known police officer and a master of ratiocination and investigation. American Fenians had been in town, with 100lbs of dynamite, coincident with the Prince's presence. Power's initiative and intuition, his determination and persistence had uncovered a Fenian plot to kill Prince George, and saved the future king's life. His tenacity had saved lives and foiled the perfidious Fenian assassins.

CHAPTER TWO

Crime and Policing in Victorian Halifax

NICHOLAS POWER was hired as a constable in the fall of 1864, the year the Halifax Police Department was created and three years before the British North America Act united the colonies in the Dominion of Canada. He retired as chief in 1907 having served 43 years, from the age of wooden ships and sail to the launch of steam turbine-powered, armoured dreadnoughts. He witnessed changes in politics, economics and society. The role of the constabulary and policing methods changed significantly. Remarkably, however, the city's bifurcated, bedrock social structure persisted, as did the nature of criminality. Policing and crime in the metropolis remained tied to certain immutable constants. This interplay between permanency—the nature of crime—and transformation—the nature of policing—provides the backdrop for Power's career.

Halifax was born of war. The strategic needs of the British Empire and the tactical demands of the Royal Navy dictated its location and the date of its establishment. The Royal Navy was its lifeblood throughout Power's career. (Power had retired by the time the Royal Navy departed and the Naval Service of Canada was created in 1910.) A picture-perfect, ice-free all year-round harbour, Halifax is also a substantial commercial port. With a significant population of transient, male, military personnel and mariners, it has always had a problematic reputation. Vices—prostitution, gambling, drunkenness—that characterise major ports of call from Hamburg to Surabaya loom large in the story of Detective Power's Halifax.

Halifax is located in the province, (former colony) of Nova Scotia, on Canada's Atlantic coast. It is 400 miles east-northeast of Boston and 3,000 miles east, across the North Atlantic, to London. It was conceived by the Royal Navy and born of the Bedford Basin. The Basin is one of the largest natural harbours in the world, second only to Sydney, Australia, and ice-free all year-round. It is roughly rectangular and approximately six miles long by three miles wide. Its gently sloping shores are ideal for the construction of berthing and transshipment facilities. Most spectacularly, it is protected by a passage known as The Narrows, a two-mile stretch of water that is less than 1,000-yards wide with an island protecting its entrance. The Narrows are dominated by a drumlin, an elongate hill composed largely of glacial deposits, on the southwestern shore, providing protection for the Basin from both enemy attack and the elements. It was chosen for the original Fort George (named after George II, the reigning monarch) and remains today the site of the present Citadel, completed in 1856, the fourth in a series of forts to sit atop what is now known as Citadel Hill. Its distinctive star shape is typical of many 19th century forts built by the British military. The Narrows' forward defenses were located at the southern tip of the peninsula on Point Pleasant.

Locals describe Halifax as a horse's head. Its northern and eastern boundaries are the Bedford Basin and The Narrows, respectively. Its southwestern boundary is the shoreline of the Northwest Arm (strangely, while the Northwest Arm is west of the city, it is south, not north, of Halifax). Extending inland three miles the Northwest Arm largely isolates Halifax from the mainland, leaving only the horse's neck at the north end of the city connecting Halifax to the remainder of the province. The Royal Navy's desire to secure the anchorage the Bedford Basin offered dictated the site of Halifax.

In the 17th century, when the British sought a foothold in the contested territory the French knew as *Acadie*, the Bedford Basin was the only logical choice—treaties and the Mi'kmaq residents be damned. And so, in 1749, Halifax was born, named in honour of George Montague-Dunk, the second Earl of Halifax, who was then President of the British Board of Trade. Its establishment triggered a savage six-year guerilla war as the resident Mi'kmaq and *Acadien* tried to force the British out of the area. They failed, the *Acadien* were expelled and Halifax became the most important Royal Navy base in the northwestern Atlantic.

The city's founder and Nova Scotia's first governor was Lieutenant General Edward Cornwallis. Fresh from suppressing Bonnie Prince Charlie's Jacobite rebellion after the battle of Culloden in 1745 and 'pacifying' the Highlands by way of burning, looting and murder, he was an arrogant, aggressive Tory. The *Acadien* could consider themselves to be lucky to be deported. Cornwallis ordered the Mi'kmaq be extirpated, going so far as to offer a bounty on Mi'kmaq scalps of ten guineas (£10 5s—approximately £1,000 today). This heinous element of his legacy has been highlighted of late.

At the south end of Barrington Street, in front of the recently restored Union (serving both the Canadian National and Canadian Pacific Railways) Station and the attached hotel, sits Cornwallis Park. In 1930 local booster and General Electric executive C H Wright persuaded the Canadian National's regional manager that a park on the land it owned, with "a statue such as that of Lord [sic] Cornwallis in front of the hotel, would immediately create an interest on the part of tourists, particular American tourists."

Subsequently, Canadian National donated the land to the city and largely funded the statue. Paths laid out in the symmetrical pattern of a Union Jack all lead to the centre of the park. At this focal point rests a massive plinth, once topped by a statue of the governor. Today, it is empty. In January 2018 the city decided that a monument celebrating a mass murdering imperialist without context was inappropriate and the statue was removed. While the green space retains the name Cornwallis Park, the fates of the statue, the plinth and future developments are currently undetermined. Statue or no statue, it remains that Halifax was established as a Royal Navy outpost, born amidst war, expulsions and genocide.

Halifax is a military town and as the military goes, so goes Halifax. War has been good to Halifax, as soldiers arrive and depart from the port, the garrison is increased, convoys assemble and the naval presence explodes. It is a boom and bust cycle. Also, like any military town issues associated with single, transient males, alcohol, gambling and prostitution are endemic, reaching epidemic proportions in wartime. In response to this situation, Halifax has always been a divided city.

Known as Lower Town, the port facilities and waterfront on the western shore of The Narrows, culminating in the Royal Navy Dockyard at the north end was largely commercial, mercantile and marine. The Upper

Streets neighbourhood, immediately below Citadel Hill and above Lower Town, was a ghetto, home to prostitutes, licensed and unlicensed purveyors of liquor by the bottle or the glass, gambling dens and the indigent. Populated by an underclass, it had a well-deserved reputation as a poverty and crime-ridden locality and was the site of the vast majority of criminal acts and activity in Halifax.

The Southside, eponymously south of South Street, on the other hand, was the stronghold of the city's privileged and influential. It was an elite that was close-knit and Anglophile, often comically so in their efforts to imitate the Royal Navy officers that regularly flowed through the upper echelons of Halifax society. Halifax social historian Judith Fingard refers to the Halifax Victorian era elite as "staid and smug". The appeal of the Southside was significantly enhanced when the British military leased the southern tip of the peninsula to the town, for a symbolic shilling *per annum* and Point Pleasant Park was created in 1866.

The Southside included Oakland Estate, owned by steamship baron Samuel Cunard. Running from Robie Street, 3,500 feet to the Northwest Arm, it boasted 2,000 feet of waterfront. It featured a gatehouse (preserved as an historic site), bathing and boat houses, a conservatory, a greenhouse, a vinery and a guest cottage. The main house, Oakland's, was Philadelphia pressed brick with freestone details set on a dressed granite foundation, with interior finishes in black walnut and oak. The Richardson Romanesque, Oland Castle was on Yonge Street (a brewery second only to Keith's, headed by the widowed family matron, Susannah). Thorndean on Inglis Street was once home to James Forman, the notorious first cashier of the Bank of Nova Scotia, who defalcated $300,000 over 40 years before he was exposed. John Thompson resided in Windsor Park at the corner of Windsor and Almon Street. Alderman, federal justice minister, Nova Scotia Supreme Court appointee and Prime Minister of Canada, as well as an eminent legal scholar, this is not the last time his name will appear in Power's story.

Sir John Sparrow David Thompson was born in 1845, the seventh and last child of Charlotte Pottinger and John Sparrow Thompson, a Methodist, teacher, journalist, editor and close friend of Father of Confederation Joseph Howe. He was educated at the Royal Acadian School and the Free Church Academy in Halifax. In 1871 he was elected as alderman for Ward 5. He made the leap to provincial politics in 1878, as the Tories unexpectedly swept to victory federally and provincially. He was appointed provincial attorney general. When a caucus revolt swept Premier Holmes from office in 1882, Thompson briefly served as Premier until the Tories lost a subsequent election. The new Liberal government immediately appointed Thompson to the provincial Supreme Court. In 1885 he made the move to federal politics and took the position of Minister of Justice, producing Canada's first Criminal Code in 1892 and, in the same year, hiring Canada's first official hangman. Sir John may be exceptional for more than the manner of his death, he died suddenly while lunching with Queen Victoria at Windsor Castle, but he is illustrative of the affluence and influence concentrated on the Southside. The Southside and the Upper streets were two solitudes.

On the rare occasions the separate spheres intersected the response was revealing. Upper Street's drunks went to the cells at the police station for the night, Police Court in the morning and, often, Rockhead Prison for supper. It was simply standard operating procedure. When the constabulary encountered "a southside lady" intoxicated in the Upper Streets she was escorted home. Noteworthy also, she was discretely not named by *The Herald*. The constabulary were loath to bring the weight of the law to bear on the elite. Their bread and butter were the soldiers and sailors, the rounders and rapscallions of the Upper Town and the waterfront. The Halifax constabulary served and protected Southside residents and Power would make his name solving the Southside burglary of the wealthy Albro clan.

While the Southside remained a bastion of wealth and privilege, overall, economically, Confederation was not kind to Halifax. It became the terminus of a spur railway with Canadian manufacturers and importers preferring cheaper and faster alternatives. In the summer the solution was simple, the port at Montreal, a shorter train trip by 750 miles. In the winter the rail connections to the ports of Boston, Massachusetts and Portland, Maine were still shorter than those to Halifax. Simply put, the superb natural harbour was not efficaciously integrated into the continental rail network.

The military establishment, a key driver of the economy, shrank after the 1860s. When Power enlisted in the newly formed Halifax Police Department in 1864, the British military presence was at its height due to Anglo-American tensions occasioned by the US Civil War. The British garrison numbered more than 5,000 and a dozen Royal Navy ships rested in the Basin. The last British troops withdrew in 1906, the year Power became chief and were replaced by a tiny Canadian contingent. The Royal Navy remained until 1910 when the newly created Royal Canadian Navy took over the Naval Dockyard. The RCN had only one unseaworthy and outdated *Diadem* class cruiser, HMCS *Niobe* in Halifax. After running aground and almost being lost on Cape Sable Island in July 1911 she was still dockside when World War One erupted in August 1914. Additionally, there were a score of cadets studying at the newly established Royal Naval College of Canada. This miniscule military commitment had a negligible impact on the local economy. It was a far cry from the historic demands of the British garrison and the Royal Navy for everything from wine, women and song to staples like food, clothing and bedding.

Over the same period wooden hulls were superseded by steel structural elements and plates sheathed with copper. Sail and rope were replaced by boilers, turbines and screws. The disappearance of these traditional trades further weakened Halifax's economy. At the dawn of the 20th century, as Nic Power reached the pinnacle of his career, Halifax was stagnating. The few manufacturers struggled, the port faced better positioned competitors and the military presence had evaporated. The city's fortunes would not improve until World War One, a decade after Power retired. Throughout the last half of the 19th century Halifax increased in population marginally, at a much slower rate than other cities in Canada, while fading in relevance economically.

On the level of criminal offences, it was a case of, 'the more things change the more they remain the same'. Inebriation was the most common offence, and the police themselves were frequently the drunkards on charge. The number increased significantly when related offences including selling alcohol without a licence, selling alcohol on Sunday and other offences, notably assaults committed by individuals under the influence were included in the total. However, murder and serious crimes were rare throughout Power's tenure. This was true across Canada. By way of illustration in 1894, when Power was at the top of his game, and one year before he was involved in multiple murder investigations, only eight murders occurred in all of Canada.

Indeed, none of the murders that Power was involved with occurred in Halifax, although many were intimately connected to the city. In 1872 the City Clerk's report noted approvingly: "It is satisfactory to know that in a population of nearly 30,000 there is such an entire absence of the higher crimes of Felony & Co, which fill the records of Police Courts of other countries, the business of our Police Court being for the most part confined to Petty Assault, Larceny and breaches of the License Law and other Bye-Laws of the City." This comment typified the era. Murder was rare, but a murder in the Maritimes that Detective Power was not involved in was rarer still. After alcohol-related offences the most common charges were forms of theft, then widely known as larceny, followed by prostitution-related violations. All are transgressions common to any port with a large garrison and naval base.

In his annual report for 1865-66, Marshall Garrett Cotter lamented: "I fear the statistics to be furnished so you will exhibit no satisfactory declension in the number of persons brought before the Police Court for drunkenness and the offences that usually arise from the excessive use of intoxicating liquors." He continued, public intoxication persisted even though "much has been done to reduce the attractions of places where liquors are sold by prohibiting music and dancing, and the use of cippi boards[1] and other like appliances for gaming."

Between October 1, 1871 and September 30, 1872, a typical one-year span, 2,304 charges were considered before the Police Court. Of these, fully 1,226 (53%) were for drunkenness. A further 62 were for violations of the Liquor Law. Furthermore, Halifax social historian Judith Fingard estimates that three-quarters of all assaults were alcohol-related, adding another 190 charges. This results in a total of 1,478 alcohol-related offences, or two-thirds of all Police Court activity. Noteworthy also is the complete absence of any serious crimes such as murder or sexual assault.

A decade later, in 1883, the marshall reported half of all convictions in 1883 were for 'drunkenness' or 'drunk and disorderly'. The remainder were a mishmash of miscellaneous, but universally mundane, offences. By way of illustration, one person was convicted of 'goats at large', two with 'smuggling dynamite', three with 'conveying liquor to prisoners' and four with 'unsound mind'.

In 1893, another decade later, the statistics had little changed. In total the Police Court adjudicated on 2,017 charges in 1893-94. Offences classified as "connected

---

1 Unable to determine what a 'cippi board' is. However, apparently they were common, as the Halifax Masonic Lodge, in 1887, decreed that its new Recreation Room include "billiard tables, cippi boards and other games, also with reading matter, and in other ways and means as the committee may see fit to make it pleasant and attractive to patrons."

with drunkenness" numbered 927, along with 107 violations of the (Liquor) License Act and 136 assaults of which, using Fingard's formula, 101 were inspired by alcohol for a total of 1,135 alcohol-related offences, or 56%. Again, there were no serious crimes such as sexual assault or murder during the year.

In the final year of Power's career two-thirds of the population of Rockhead Prison had been convicted of alcohol-related offences and more than half of all offences adjudicated by the Police Court involved alcohol. Visitors to the city opined that half of the population of Halifax was drunk and the other half was engaged in the selling of rum. This report from *The Herald*, dated August 3, 1887 is typical: "A fat old sea dog from the US warship *Osippe* [*sic*] was charged with being drunk and incapable. He pleaded guilty, informing the magistrate that he hadn't got the gauge of liquor sold down this way... Three other sailors from the same ship were charged with being drunk and sleeping on a wharf. All of them were sent below and an officer of the ship notified." The USS *Osippee* (named after the river in Maine) was a wooden, steam-powered, screw-driven man of war that served on the North Atlantic station from 1873 to 1878. Throughout the period, constantly and consistently, alcohol-related crimes comprised a majority of all offences while serious crime was minimal.

A frequent offence that seems on its face unlikely, related to youths blocking sidewalks. However, the sidewalks were not concrete alongside paved streets. They consisted of wooden duckboards alongside muddy streets, the mire consisting of an admixture of dirt and manure. For women wearing long skirts, and the sake of everyone's footwear, to be forced off the sidewalk was a serious inconvenience.

Detectives, both Power and his predecessor William Hutt, were involved in prominent cases of larceny, fraud and murder throughout the region. However, it would be a mistake to assume that their sole responsibility was detection. When they were in the city, they often accompanied officers on the beat, strolled and patrolled the city in their civilian attire and engaged in routine matters of policing. Power participated in liquor licensing violation raids and he often appears as the arresting officer for a host of minor offences. An interesting episode from October 1885 serves to illustrate Power's intimate involvement in the nitty-gritty of 19th century policing. On October 26 of that year, Constable Foley ended up worse for wear after an altercation with Henry Mclure, a local hooligan with a long criminal record. Mclure wrestled Foley's baton away from him and struck him in the head three times, knocking him senseless and cutting him severely. Responding, Power pursued Mclure across the Halifax Common, arresting him after finding him passed out in a barn. Even as a detective Power responded to assaults on fellow officers in uniform and endured the never-ending routine of arresting inebriants. Standing six feet, four inches and towering over his contemporaries,

Power never carried a weapon, but was always willing and able to mix it up.

In 1888 Detective Power found his considerable bulk confronting a pip squeak of a sneak thief. Watches were disappearing from ships alongside the city's wharves. Power's investigation revealed they had been pawned by a teenaged Newfoundlander, Thomas Brine, who was promptly arrested. *The Herald* had nothing good to say about the young gonoph and his kin: "Brine is very small for his age. He is the oldest of two saucy youngsters… They are both bad boys and belong to a bad family. The keeper of the notorious dive on Duke Street, recently broken up by police, is a sister of theirs." From violent drunks to juvenile sneak thieves, Nic Power had to stoop to conquer when he was not making headlines chasing embezzlers and notorious murderers.

The prosaic nature of most policing is captured by the subjects of Mayor James C Mackintosh's October 1884 address to the department. The mayor, formerly a Bank of Nova Scotia bean counter, was the man who brought Forman's massive defalcation to light. His address highlighted: "Prevention of attacks on and insults to females at night, stopping defacement of property and injury of shade trees, detections of sales of light bread, unlicensed liquor selling, unlicensed dogs, cleaning snow from sidewalks, young girls on the streets at night misbehaving themselves, minors smoking… swearing and prowling about in the suburbs disturbing the peace and comfort of citizens." The typical Halifax constable spent his dreary days rousting drunks and loiterers, arresting the demimonde, breaking up fights and collaring petty thieves.

Prior to the establishment of the Halifax Police Department in 1864, public order was maintained by a dozen paid day constables and a 12-man, permanent, volunteer night watch, all overseen by the city marshall. The growth of the town, coupled with the elevated numbers of naval personnel, civilian sailors and transients common to any port, all exacerbated by the American Civil War, increased the demand for prostitutes, gambling dens and libations. These threats to public order led the city to formally establish the Halifax Police Department in 1864. Its members were "expected to be sober, intelligent, trustworthy, orderly and athletic, and to place themselves and all those qualities at the disposal of the city."

Marshall Garrett Cotter remained as head of the new police department. His annual report to the Town Council, submitted December 7, 1866, provides a picture of the Police Department at its inception. It had a total budget of $15,540, representing 22% of the total town budget of $72,000. Under the marshall and his deputy were six sergeants of police and 30 policemen, in all 38 men. The marshall received a salary of $800, his deputy $560. The six sergeants of police earned $400 and the lowly constables were paid $360 (the equivalent of less than $20,000 US today). It would be 1872 before Marshall Cotter called for a raise from the Police Committee. The

Police Department did not have in its employ a detective, but its budget allocated $100 to detective services and a final $200 to the 'Keeper of Lockup'.

The marshall outlined in detail the men's organisation and deployment:

> Three sergeants and 15 policemen perform duty on the streets during the night, commencing at 8 o'clock pm and ending at 6 o'clock am the following morning. Two sergeants and nine policemen perform duty on the streets during the day, commencing at 8 o'clock am and ending at 6 o'clock pm. One sergeant and five policemen are detailed for office duty; two men of this division are in attendance at the police station in succession, night and day to take charge of prisoners. One policeman is detailed as special messenger for the Mayor's Office... It is the duty of each policeman to appear at certain corners every hour, so as to answer to his sergeant and the call of any citizen who may require his service.

He then reminded all and sundry, "the members of the Department have been regularly inspected monthly by His Worship the Mayor and the members of the Police Committee, and complimented on each occasion for their efficiency and creditable appearance." All serving to justify his opening assurance that "it gives me great pleasure to assure you that the Police Department are in a state of efficiency—second to no city of its size on this Continent..."

By 1880 salaries for all had risen somewhat. The marshall's salary increased by more than 25% to $1,080 and by 1883 it would be $1,200. Two deputy marshalls received $630 each, rising to $700 by 1883, while sergeants and policemen received small raises. The full-time city detective, William Hutt, was paid a salary of $540, 20% more than a sergeant, he also wore mufti and, accordingly, received an annual clothing allowance variously described as $40 or one suit. By 1883, Power's first full year as a detective, the salary was $600, and the overall Police Department budget had grown to $21,601.83.

The 1879-80 City Marshall's Report notes that the Police Department stands now at 40, an addition of only two men in 15 years, and a slight reduction from the most recent years, despite the growth of the city. According to the 1861 Census the population of Halifax was 25,026, two decades later it had grown to 36,100, an increase of 45%, while the Police Department had increased by only 5%. With the population increase the city had also grown geographically and in no sense had the Police Department kept pace.

The report details how these resources are deployed:

> The department at present consists of a marshall, deputy marshall, assistant deputy marshall, detective, six sergeants of police and 30 policemen—in all 40 men. The sergeant and men are detailed as follows:

DAY DUTY

Two sergeants and 11 men distributed as follows: One sergeant and seven men north of Jacob Street, and a sergeant and four men south of Jacob, the western parts of the city north and south being included in these distributions. The sergeant and four men are on duty at the office daily, two doing duty at the station at night in rotation.

NIGHT DUTY

A sergeant and four men from Inglis Street to Sackville Street, including the western part of the city between Inglis and Sackville streets; a sergeant and four men from Sackville Street to Jacob Street, and a sergeant and six men from Jacob Street to Wellington Barracks and Richmond Depot.

In his 1872 report, Marshall Cotter, for the first time referred to the importance of an investigator noting: "During the past year Sergeant Hutt has been almost exclusively employed in detective duty." He went on to outline the benefits to the department of having at its disposal a detective. "It has been found essential to have an officer at hand, to whom may be entrusted matters sometimes requiring the exercise of great prudence and ingenuity... but which are beyond the ordinary routine of police duty. Through this means a large amount of stolen property has been restored to the owners, and much information obtained which has frequently proved of the highest importance." This quote implies that deterrence and not detection was regarded as 'routine' police duty, but that detection is a cat of a different colour, and one growing in importance.

The importance of stolen property 'restored to owners' is significant, although it will seem strange to the modern reader. The Police Department collected a percentage of the value of restored property when the owner was made whole through the return of his property. It is reported regularly in Halifax's annual financial statements and is noted specifically in the marshall's annual reports. In his 1873 report, Marshall Cotter again asserted the importance of Detective Hutt pointing out: "Considerable stolen property has been recovered by him. The necessity for such an officer in connection with the Police Department is becoming more apparent every day." In October 1882, Detective Hutt departed this mortal coil causing "a vacancy in that department, which was filled up by the City Council by the appointment of Sergeant Power to that position."

The Marshall's Report for Nicholas Power's first year as a detective notes the value, in cold hard cash, of his detective work. "A large amount of valuable stolen property has been returned to the respective owners. The amount earned and received for his services since his appointment, in October last, is two hundred and thirty-eight dollars, which was paid over to the City Clerk, and by him paid into the City Treasury." Two years later he almost doubled that figure. "The receipts from this Department amount to four hundred and thirty-five dollars." Detection padded the bottom line.

Alternately, receipts can be seen as the detective subsidising his own salary. In 1884 Power received a salary of $600 and an additional clothing allowance of $40. Against this total cost he earned $435 in receipts, for a net cost of only $205, less than a mere constable, and a bargain at twice the price. With limited taxation powers and revenues, municipal governments were notoriously parsimonious in Power's era and the 'earning' power of Detective Power would not have gone unnoticed.

While the report identified many positives, notably the profitability of a detective, it also revealed an increasingly dysfunctional department. It could not keep its employees. "Two sergeants and 17 men have ceased to be members of the Department (this year—1884). Of these, one sergeant and one private were dismissed; one private died, one sergeant and 14 privates resigned; and one private deserted. Of the privates who resigned, more than one, by so doing, only anticipated the action of the Committee." Half of the Police Committee's 10 meetings in 1872 "were devoted chiefly against investigation of charges against members of the Department" and the vast majority of these dealt with drunkenness. Over and over again members of the force are alleged to have reported for duty drunk, been drunk on duty or to have been seen drinking in uniform and on duty. Moreover, substantiated evidence of repeated incidents of being drunk on duty was not necessarily grounds for dismissal.

The crescendo of Policeman Haggarty's career captures this reluctance. On November 24, 1885 the Police Committee demanded his resignation after repeated discipline for being drunk on duty. On December 15 he was again before the committee for having been drunk on duty on November 29. The commission determined to dismiss him if he did not resign immediately. A week later, still in uniform, he was again charged with being drunk on duty, a charge that was overlooked "because it was Christmas time the Committee relent." On January 29, 1886, he admitted to being drunk on duty "but pleads that he was sick and took liquor as a medicine" and the committee deferred action. Finally, the besotted Haggarty resigned on Friday, February 5, 1886.

Two years later, Policeman Inglis commenced a five-year period littered with offences before he was finally dismissed. On June 29, 1888, the Friday night of the Dominion Day holiday weekend, Policeman Inglis was accused by the Third Officer of HMS *Hinna*, of being drunk and refusing to take a prisoner into custody. Sergeant Nickerson also accused Inglis of being drunk on duty and of challenging him to a fight. Remarkably, the committee dismissed all charges. Inglis seems to have had a thing for holidays and something against soldiers. Two days after New Year's Day 1889, several soldiers of the West Riding Regiment accused him of "being drunk and unnecessarily interfering with them on the streets of the city." The minutes of the meeting conclude, "No action is taken."

On April 16, Sergeant Condon charges Inglis with again being drunk on duty four days earlier. According to *The Herald,* at one point Inglis was so inebriated he fell off a chair. The committee finally acts. It suspends Inglis, but passes the ball to the council as a whole regarding his dismissal. A heated debate ensues. Alderman Keefe moved an amendment to the dismissal motion adding a $10 fine. In a long speech, the chairman of the Police Committee, Alderman Charles H Smith, Ward 2, identified the root of the problem. "When a policeman is reported they go to their friends and the friends button hole the aldermen, and the offence is but lightly punished." Cronyism meant existing policies were not being enforced and, apparently, Inglis had friends in high places. Both the motion to dismiss him and the amendment to also fine him were defeated. He was still wearing the blue in August when a Mrs P E Whelan accused him "of having used abusive language against her", earning him a reprimand. She levelled a second accusation of abusive language against Inglis on October 27. On the same day Sergeant Nickerson again accused him of being drunk on duty. Inglis escaped even a slap on the wrist. Mrs Whelan's charge is dismissed "because it resulted from a private altercation between Mrs Whelan's family and Inglis." The response to the charge of drunkenness is a repeat performance. "An amendment to merely fine him $10 is defeated (No action taken on the dismissal)."

Finally, he was suspended in January 1890 after facing another drunk on duty charge. Reinstated as a 'special policeman', he resumed limited duties. Six months later the committee recommended that he be fully reinstated with a firm warning that "any breach of the police regulations on his part will be followed by immediate dismissal." Three years later he finally ran out of rope and, following the department's shake up in 1892, he was dismissed by newly installed Chief O'Sullivan. These two dipsomaniacs' careers clearly indicate that misbehaviour, particularly drunkenness, was hardly a bar to a career as a Halifax policeman. As historian David McGahan delicately puts it, "not all were suited for the routine and discipline of police work." Power was the department's bad detective, but Inglis can claim the crown as its worst policeman.

Alderman Smith's accusations of cronyism and political interference in the department are borne out by an incident in the spring of 1884. Constable Daniel Brechnor testified against a sergeant on the department who was accused of assaulting a prisoner. The sergeant's attorney, William F MacCoy, of MacCoy & Morrison, put Brechnor through the wringer during his cross-examination, but could not shake his story. As Brechnor left the stand, MacCoy passed him a note and asked him to deliver it to Marshall Cotter. Brechnor read the note and handed it to the plaintiff's attorney, C Sidney Harrington, who read it to the court. "To the City Marshall, Daniel Brechnor has been very impertinent to me and I require him to be suspended until investigation. Signed, W F MacCoy." At the time MacCoy was not just a barrister, he was both an alderman and a member of the police committee. A more blatant example of political interference in the department would be hard to find.

But it was not impossible, not in Halifax. Two years later, after an incident involving disruptive Sunday drunks, *The Herald* asked Sergeant Nickerson why charges had not been entered in the charge book at the station. He helpfully explained that the local Ward 5 alderman, grocer and feed store owner, John T Ead, had ordered him not to do so. Prodded by *The Herald*, Nickerson laid the charge, but no summons was issued. *The Herald* persevered, "enquiries were duly made of the city clerk as to why the process had not issued when it was learned that Alderman Ead had again decreed the law by ordering that the summons should not issue; and that it was the second time that he had interfered to prevent the law dealing with a violation of the license act by Mrs Woods." Clearly, political protection could shield lawbreakers and impair guardians' careers or, as McGahan tactfully notes: "The Halifax guardians did not function in a political vacuum."

In the early 1890s dissatisfaction with the performance

of the police was reflected in a major revamp of the department's organisation, administration and operation. There are two ways to view this exercise. On the one hand, there must have been problems or reorganisation would not have been on the table. On the other hand, it can hardly be deemed unusual that almost 30 years after its formation an organisation required restructuring. Another motive, more ceremonial, may also have been at play. Preparing to move into new digs in the basement of the impressive new City Hall, a corresponding organisational renovation may have seemed apropos. The precipitating incident was the death of a young prisoner, in the "inhuman, indecent and dangerous" (according to a *Herald* correspondent) cells in the basement of the old police station on Spring Garden Road. Exacerbating the tragedy, and the embarrassment of the department, was the unfortunate timing of the death, Christmas Eve, 1891. With the prisoner's death, voices demanding change in the department reached a crescendo.

In January 1892 a correspondent to the *Herald* identified only as 'Citizen' outlined the problems with the department. "Our public thoroughfares are daily, not excepting occasionally even Sunday, taken possession of by gangs of boys and made playgrounds of... Vandalism is rampant." Citizen also accused the constabulary of neglecting their duty, choosing instead to "while away their time in engine-houses, perchance in a friendly game of enchretor[2] or in dilating in some crispin's [a shoemaker, after St Crispin, the patron saint of shoemakers] shop on the merits of a bull pup, or the latest scandal of the police court, or in a barber's shop taking lessons in the tonsorial art." In a nutshell, Citizen accused the constabulary of being lax in enforcing the law and lazy in the execution of their duty. In October, *The Herald* condemned the Police Committee and civic government of Halifax for detaching officers from policing to attend to social and civic responsibilities. "It is said that 11 men are off duty, six or seven having been detached from regular duty for six weeks to take the school census. It strikes most people that all the policemen ought to be on police duty so that the law can be rigidly enforced and public order maintained." In a similar vein, the Police Committee dismissed an appeal to enforce the Truancy Act. By 1892 the department wanted to focus on crime, investigation and solution, not social services.

Additionally, the term revitalisation is particularly apt as the issue seems to have been age as much as organisation and operation. At the time Marshall Cotter was 72 years old, having served as a Halifax peace officer for 50 years. Deputy Marshall McDonald was of a similar vintage. On March 29, 1893 Halifax council approved a sweeping reorganisation of the police department.

---

2 Despite extensive research and inquiry, I have no idea what game this refers to.

Both the marshall and his deputy were removed from leadership roles in the department. McDonald was superannuated at a rate of $400 annually. Marshall Cotter retained his title, but his responsibilities were limited to the civil courts at an annual salary of $800. In the same vein the oldest constables and sergeants were assigned to strictly office duties. Restricting the oldest, least physically fit officers to paperwork, freed up younger officers more capable of walking a beat. Shedding social service roles gave these young bucks more time to collar criminals.

A new position, that of Chief of Police, was created at an annual salary of $1,000 with annual increases of $100 to a maximum of $1,300. Sergeant John O'Sullivan, a 28-year veteran, was promoted, becoming the first Chief of Police. Sergeant Nickerson was appointed his deputy. Oversight of the department was also altered. The Police Committee of Council was replaced by a Police Commission comprised of the mayor, the Chief of Police and one alderman.

The Herald greeted the changes with optimism. On May 23, 1893, reporting on the new Police Commissioner's first meeting with the department it stated: "The men were charged not to enter any liquor saloons for drinks… They were told to keep clean and tidy at all times… To obey promptly all orders given by the chief… To watch all licensed houses, billiard saloons, disorderly houses and houses of ill-repute on their beats." New overseers, new organisation and new leadership all promised a fresh start.

Alas, the yearning for sunny ways went unfilled. In July of that year the new Police Commission found itself dealing with an old problem, the guardians' misbehaviour. Notably, Officer Inglis was dismissed for being intoxicated while on duty, provoking an interesting test of the new administrative structure. Inglis appealed to the City Council for reinstatement. Council responded that it no longer had any authority over the police through the Police Committee of Council and, therefore, had no jurisdiction over the decisions of the independent Police Commission. While Inglis' career was not resurrected, the independence of the Police Commission was firmly established.

It only took two months for cynicism to set in. A correspondent to *The Herald* on July 27 lamented: "I am very much inclined to the idea that the change has been anything but beneficial or in the public interest." He dismissed the recent commission's meeting as a 'festival'. Regardless, O'Sullivan would remain chief for almost 15 years and the commission was here to stay.

Throughout this period, the growing importance, and value, of a detective was reflected in his salary growth at a rate far greater than that of the uniformed officers. In 1879 the detective's salary was set at $540. It reached $600 in 1882, the year Power was promoted to the rank. In 1888 it increased to $700. Two years later it increased again to $800, along with a $40 allowance for clothing. The detective's salary progressively increased throughout

Power's career. Noteworthy also, in 1905, he joined the chief, as the only two members of the department with home telephones included in the department budget.

Most important, in terms of Power's career, is the diverse and disparate nature of his detecting career. While major crimes are notably rare during this period in Halifax, that does not mean that Power was not busy. As the only detective on any police department in the Maritimes he was often on the road, called to other jurisdictions by order of the provincial Attorney General or at the request of local authorities.

By way of illustration, none of the four cases at the core of this story occurred in Halifax, although one was, in part, investigated there. Those three murders occurred on the high seas and a killing of four happened on Cape Breton Island, the easternmost point in the province. The other two happened near the Bay of Fundy coast, north of Halifax, in the rural hamlet of Bear River and the small town of Plympton. This wide field of operations, coupled with his assignment to only the most serious and sensational crimes, made Power an appealing subject for the newspapers. Most Halifax police officers spent their days rousting drunks, enforcing liquor regulations and dealing with the familiar faces of recidivists in the Upper Streets, but not Detective Nicholas Power and it was more than mufti that distinguished him. His job was not prevention but rather detection, and that calling was about to become all the rage.

CHAPTER THREE

The Age of the Super Sleuth

PHILATELISTS HONOUR May 6, 1840 as the birth date of the Penny Black, the world's first adhesive postage stamp. Its introduction was one of two reforms that revolutionised the English postal system. Prior to 1840 the post was disorganised, fragmented and costly. Notably, the sender of a letter did not pay the postage, the recipient did. If the postman knocked at the door and the required coins were not immediately forthcoming, the missive was not delivered. Expensive, but slow and unreliable, it was held in low regard.

Rowland Hill was a schoolmaster and disgruntled user of the postal system. Tirelessly, on his own time, he ruminated on the problem and developed an outrageous, outside the box, solution. After a long public campaign and extensive lobbying, he was authorised to execute his proposed changes. The prepaid postage stamp was introduced and the sender, not the recipient, assumed responsibility for postage. This eliminated the inconvenience of immediate payment upon receipt. Secondly, as the stamp's moniker declares, the price was slashed to one penny for any envelope weighing less than half an ounce. Hill predicted that the lower price would be made up for by increased volume. He was right. The number of letters posted doubled in the first year and again by the end of the decade. Nova Scotia issued its first postage stamps, denominated in pence and shillings in 1851, with a second issue a dozen years later in the decimal system with values ranging from one cent to 12½ cents. By 1865 more than 90 countries had adopted his system and were issuing prepaid adhesive postage stamps. American research indicates that postal reforms fostered further innovation. Interestingly, the number of patent applications is linked to the proximity and density of postal outlets in a given area. As the postal system develops the number of patent applications increases. Despite snail mail's recent decline, it was an influential channel of communication for 150 years and, at its introduction, Hill's system revolutionised communication within Great Britain.

The next day, Thursday, May 7, 1840 it was neither the Penny Black nor Rowland Hill in the headlines. True to the principle 'if it bleeds it leads' it was murder, the savage murder of Lord William Russell. The whiff of youthful scandal, a peripatetic lifestyle and a plethora of odd personal habits marked an otherwise forgettable life, exceptional only for the violence of his death. His throat had been slit so savagely that he was effectively decapitated. A gash, seven inches long and five inches deep had severed the trachea. It appeared a botched robbery had led to the murder. A murder all the more frightening because it occurred on Norfolk Street, only steps from the northeast corner of Hyde Park, in Mayfair, the most exclusive residential neighbourhood in London. Queen Victoria, barely 20, wrote in her diary: "This is really too horrid. It is almost an unparalleled thing for a person of Lord William's rank to be killed like that." She feared it was a political assassination, revenge for the 22 members of the Chartist Movement shot by troops in Newport in Monmouthshire the previous November.

The victim was the third, and youngest son of the Marquess of Tavistock, doomed, by his late arrival, to a life of indolent affluence. Through four elections he held the family's rotten borough of Tavistock, often passing years abroad and rarely speaking in the House of Lords. He was consistently overshadowed by his elder brothers, Francis Russell, the 5th Duke of Bedford, and John Russell, the 6th Duke of Bedford, his nephew Francis Russell, the 7th Duke of Bedford and a second nephew, the future Prime Minister Lord John Russell (who was Colonial Secretary at the time of the murder).

In the wake of his marriage in 1789 his wife Charlotte inspired gossip with her dalliances with the Duke of Argyll. Diarist Elizabeth Wynne, after dining with the Russells and the Duke of Argyll, wrote of Lord William: "*Quoiqu'il me paraît un zéro dans sa maison*" (He is nothing in his own home). Charlotte died in 1808 and since then Lord Russell had led a rootless and largely solitary life. Couch-surfing in an elegant Regency style befitting his class, living in hotels and leaving town if it was rumoured relatives might be visiting, he continued to spend most of his time in Europe.

In 1840, over the age of 70, his travelling days behind him, he had settled into his Georgian townhouse spending his days at his clubs, Brook's on St James's Street and the Traveller's on Pall Mall, returning home to a solitary dinner and an evening of reading. He kept only a small household staff—a maid, Sarah Mancer; a valet, newly hired with excellent references, François Benjamin Courvoisier; and a cook, Mary Hannell. A coachman and a groom lived offsite in the Mews and the carriage was stored around the corner at Shenton's livery stable. Lord Russell's eccentricities included pacing with his large pocket watch in his mouth and he had a reputation for being a grouchy, demanding employer. Hardly grounds for homicide however.

On the morning of May 6, the maid, arising first, discovered the topsy-turvy state of the ground floor and sought out the valet, Courvoisier. Together they ventured into Lord Russell's bedchamber. Courvoisier proceeded directly to open the curtains and it was left to Mancer to discover their murdered master. Hysterically, she raced into the street, screaming and banging on adjacent doors she roused the neighbourhood in a quest for help, a doctor or a 'Peeler', a constable (latterly known as 'Bobbies', both nicknames derived from their founder's name Robert Peel).

The scene gave the appearance of a botched robbery. A sac of plate, silver and other valuables sat on the floor; drawers, buffets and bureaus on the main floor had been ransacked, the service entrance into the pantry below the front door appeared to have been forced and the unlatched front door gave evidence of an escape route. Incongruous aspects of the crime scene led investigators to suspect the appearance of a robbery had been staged. Blame soon focused on the Swiss valet, Courvoisier. Missing household valuables were found secreted in his room and he was arrested. During the run-up to the trial Courvoisier's attorney attempted to shift the blame to the maid, Sarah Mancer. Refusing to implicate her, at this point Courvoisier confessed, truthfully or not, that he, and he alone was responsible for the pilfering of silver and other property, and the murder. He was duly sentenced to death.

Withdrawing his previous confession following a long interview with his uncle Louis, butler to Sir George Howland Beaumont, the 9th Baronet of Stoughton Grange, he asked to see Sheriff Evans. He retracted his previous confession of a burglary interrupted and offered a second, 'true' confession. *The Examiner* (London), an influential, radical Sunday weekly, reported Courvoisier "declared, and he wished the Sheriff to let it be known to the world, that the idea was first suggested to him by reading and seeing a performance of Jack Sheppard." (Published in 1839 and promptly taken to the stage). The book containing the story of Jack Sheppard had been "lent to him by one of the servants of the Duke of Bedford, and he lamented that he had ever seen it." The condemned man was blaming his fall from grace on a work of fiction. *The Examiner*, noting Courvoisier "ascribes his crimes to perusal of that detestable book, *Jack Sheppard*", opined "certainly it is a publication calculated to familiarise the mind with cruelties, and to serve as the cutthroat's manual, or the midnight assassin's *vade mecum* [pocket manual]..." When *The Times* adopted a similar editorial stance, public hysteria skyrocketed and a moral panic erupted, such that the author, W H Ainsworth, denied his 'romance' had any relationship to the crime in letters to both *The Times* and the *Morning Chronicle* (London). This prompted Sheriff Evans to respond with his own letter affirming Courvoisier "did assert to me that 'the idea of murdering his master was first suggested to him by a perusal of the book called *Jack Sheppard*.'"

Two of England's leading novelists found themselves on opposite sides of the issue. Charles Dickens, whose fourth novel, *The Old Curiosity Shop,* had just started appearing in his own journal, *Master Humphrey's Clock*, believed Courvoisier guilty, and his lawyer a shyster. William Makepeace Thackeray, regarded the carnival of interest as glorifying criminals, both Courvoisier and Sheppard. However, in Courvoisier he saw a victim of the *Jack Sheppard* mania. His first novel, *Catherine: A Story* had wrapped up serialised publication in *Fraser's Magazine* only months before the murder. He wrote it as an antidote to what he saw as the corrosive moral influence of *Jack Sheppard* and the entire genre known at the time as Newgate novels. This case, the role of a novel and the intimate involvement of novelists, serves as a springboard to a discussion of the strange interplay of truth and fiction; yellow journalism and the popular obsession with murder; and, newspapermen and detectives that characterised Power's era. Together they created a fervid atmosphere around murder and detection that, combined with Power's boundless self-confidence and media savvy, gave birth to the myth of Canada's Sherlock Holmes.

Jack Sheppard is a Newgate novel, an antecedent of the detective novel, dealing with the underworld and convicts (Newgate Prison, at the corner of Newgate Street and the Old Bailey took in its first prisoners in 1188 and was demolished in 1904). Titillating the middle class was the focus of this genre, not detection, and clumsy use of underworld slang characterised the dialogue. It was a Victorian version of the hardboiled novel or *roman noir* that characterised Dashiell Hammett's work. In Hammett's *The Maltese Falcon* the precipitating murder of private dick Sam Spade's partner, Miles Archer, is the mystery demanding investigation. It is never solved and detection takes a back seat to pursuit of the illusive statuette. In a similar fashion, his first novel *Red Harvest* details a nameless Continental Op's efforts to covertly start a gang war, not detection. Newgate novels and American hardboiled fiction depict criminals and the criminal underworld, not detectives and investigation. Despite its shortcomings it was a popular genre in the early years of Queen Victoria's reign and the star of the genre was Jack Sheppard.

In reality, Jack Sheppard was a remarkably unsuccessful, 18th century thief. He was arrested five times in a criminal career that spanned less than two years. However, he was arrested so frequently because he repeatedly escaped. Four times he broke out of prison and resumed his larcenous behaviour. There was not a fifth escape because a warder found the hidden pen knife he intended to use to cut his bonds and slip the noose on the way to the gallows. His repeated escapes and his refusal to accept a commutation predicated on betraying his confederates made him a folk hero in the 19th century. Despite having been executed over a century earlier, in November 1724, at the young age of 22, he was undergoing a renaissance when Lord William was murdered in 1840. The year before, popular novelist William Harrison Ainsworth, published a highly fictionalised biography, *Jack Sheppard*, that told a romantic tale of a noble figure. Its first installments appeared in *Bentley's Miscellany* alongside the final installments of Dickens' *Oliver Twist*, another best-seller about the criminal underclass. *Jack Sheppard* immediately became wildly popular.

In an era before refined copyright law popularity inspired flattery in the form of imitation in countless knock-offs. There was an 'official' version for the stage that appeared beside numerous unauthorised productions in London and the provinces. Newsboys hawked broadsides with sketches of Jack, his crimes, escapes and execution on street corners. Ballads and laments were written and sung. Itinerant entertainers did up their wagons with grisly illustrations, augmenting the display with artifacts, undoubtedly spurious, from the thefts and escapes, and perhaps even a purported death mask. They then ambled through small towns charging a penny for a view of the shocking display. Madame Tussaud's added a tableau of the murder to its ever-popular display of young Jack Sheppard escaping. Ainsworth's *Jack Sheppard* made Jack Sheppard a cultural meme. After the publication of the eponymous novel, *Jack Sheppard*, in a decidedly 19th century manner, the young ne'er-do-well became a meme, omnipresent in every form and style of entertainment then popular.

Along with the hardboiled Newgate novels, sensation novels were also popular at the time. They often focused also on crime, but not the criminality of the urban underworld. Finding their protagonists in more rarefied classes and focusing on issues of identity—infants switched at birth, a secret previous marriage or forged wills and documents—they also emerged mid-century. They represent a distinctly separate stream from the detective novel. The sensation novels focused on the back story, a secret from the past explained the characters' behaviour and its revelation offered resolution. In this sense they look back, turning to the past to explain the events of the present.

With a shift in focus but not setting or *dramatis personae* these two genres gave birth to the detective novel. In contrast to the earlier forms, the detective novel is forward-looking and past secrets do not resolve the mystery. Resolution is only achieved by the detective looking forward, investigating, employing clues to assemble a narrative of events and identifying the culprit. The reader looks forward to a solution, the answers are not to be found in the past. This type of novel was as popular in British North America as it was in England. Disregarding British copyright, cheap reprints of British fiction proliferated in North America. The detective novel quickly became a bestseller on both sides of the Atlantic.

Looking for historical firsts is usually a mug's game. Few firsts are as definite as the issuance of the 'Penny Black' or Neil Armstrong's 'giant leap for mankind' (assuming one dismisses the conspiracy theory that the entire episode was filmed on the acid rain-swept rock of northern Ontario's barren Canadian Shield). Such is the case with the first detective fiction. Literary critics and historians debate the birth of detective fiction. What can be said with certainty is that between the publication of Edgar Allen Poe's short story 'Murders in the Rue Morgue' in 1841, arguably the first tale of ratiocination and *The Moonstone* (1868), Wilkie Collins' door-stopper about a purloined and cursed yellow diamond, the detective story was 'invented'. In Halifax, by the 1880s the link between crime and crime novels merited an editorial in *The Herald* dismissing the prevailing opinion. "It is impossible to believe that it [the dime novel] has inspired quite as many murders and burglaries as alleged, that it has transformed multitudes of innocent boys and girls into demoniac manikins, or laid the foundation of a career of adult crime in every infantile mind interested in its thrilling details." That the connection merited discussion and dismissal speaks to how widespread it must have been.

The genre's popularity exploded with Conan Doyle's creation of Sherlock Holmes. *A Study in Scarlet*, Holmes' first appearance, was a moderately successful novel. Holmes as a cultural phenomenon arose with the publication of 'A Scandal in Bohemia', a short story in *The Strand* magazine in 1891. Holmes is purportedly the most filmed character in history and fan conventions organised by 'The Baker Street Irregulars', the all-male fan club, and the female-only 'Baker Street Babes' convene annually. Sherlock Holmes personifies the detective as a late-Victorian meme. Power's career parallels the fictional detective's rising star. The same readers that marvelled at Holmes' fictional adventures devoured the 'yellow' press that claimed to chronicle Power's real-life, investigative exploits. This fanaticism developed fast and furiously fed by, and fuelling, the popular obsession with true crime's resolution by an erudite investigator known as a scientific or consulting detective, as Holmes referred to himself.

Such was not always the case, nor, however, is it new news (as is also the case with fake news). If 'it bleeds, it leads' was as true of the yellow press 125 years ago as it is today. While the Victorians added a sense of urgency to their obsession with murderous violence, the human fascination with murder is age old. However, the manner in which it was manifest in the late-Victorian age was in many ways remarkable. There was an unusual interplay between fact and fiction, reporters and detectives, novelists and criminals, and other stakeholders. A focus on investigation in the person of the scientific detective employing both logic, erudition and the ability to spot a clue overlooked by others, grew. This was true in fact, commencing in 1842 detectives were on the roster of the Metropolitan Police in London and shortly after the creation of the Halifax Police Department, William Hutt was promoted to the newly created rank of detective. In fiction, Poe, Collins, Conan Doyle and others made it equally true.

The origin of the noun detective is instructive. Its classical roots lie in the Latin verb, *tegere*—to cover, and the prefix *de*—expressing reversal, producing *detegere*—to uncover. It passed into late Middle English as the verb detect. It was not until 1840 that it morphed into an adjective. The *Oxford English Dictionary* credits the shift to *Chamber's Magazine* in 1843: "Intelligent men have been recently selected to form a body called the 'detective police'... at times the detective policeman attires himself in the dress of ordinary individuals."

The *Oxford English Dictionary* traces the shift from an adjective to a noun to 1850. It credits it to William Henry Wills' essay 'The modern science of thief-taking', published in the July 13 issue of *Household Words*, edited by Charles Dickens: "To each division of the Force is attached two officers, who are denominated 'detectives'." Surprisingly, the *Oxford English Dictionary* attributes a late birth to the term 'detective novel', 1924. Yet, in May 1863 the *Englishwoman's Domestic Magazine* remarked on the popularity of stories "called 'detective' novels', which place the reader in the position of a Bow Street Runner, panting and breathless to join in the 'hue and cry', and to run down imaginary crime." Etymological arcana aside, it was only at the middle of the 19th century, as Power's police career commenced, that detective began to flourish in the English language and the

English-speaking world's psyche. Samuel Taylor Coleridge wrote: "Language is the armoury of the human mind, and at once contains the trophies of its past and the weapons of its future conquests." Detective work was one of policing's 'weapons of its future conquests'. Words are the building blocks of language and the significance of the etymological emergence of detective cannot be overstated.

With detective and detective novel joining the lexicon, the establishment of a Detective Bureau at the London Metropolitan Police, and the extraordinary popularity of Sherlock Holmes, the ascent of the detective was complete, and the cultural stage was set for scientific detective Nicholas Power. Power's career as a detective corresponded with the invention of murder[3] and the ascent of the detective.[4] He investigated his cases amid a perfect storm of interest in detection, hysterical popular press attention and a popular fixation on murder, the more lurid the better. A strange brew of social and cultural trends converged to generate an obsession with murder and mayhem and a fascination with the detective who solved these mysteries and assured the victory of the forces of order and stability. Detective Power would

---

3 Judith FLANDERS. *The Invention of Murder: How the Victorians Revelled in Death and Detection and Created Modern Crime* Harper Press: 2011.

4 Haia SHPAYER-MAKOV. *The Ascent of the Detective: Police Sleuths in Victorian and Edwardian England* Oxford University Press: 2011.

arrive on the scene at the very moment when the public was primed for a larger than life, heroic, scientific detective. He was perfectly cast and would prove more than willing to take a star turn.

At the same time as the public was becoming enamoured with detection, policing was undergoing significant changes in organisation, operations and methods. The origins of Halifax policing in Power's era lie across the Atlantic and the ages in Hanoverian England. Established by magistrate and novelist Henry Fielding in 1749 and supervised for years by his blind, half-brother John, the Bow Street Runners were themselves successors to the thief-takers of the 17th and 18th centuries. Thief-takers ran down criminals for private citizens who had hired them to do so and to claim rewards offered for the return of stolen property or the apprehension of thieves. These financial arrangements created an incentive to capture a culprit, guilty or not, in order to claim the reward. Other thief-takers happily acted as middlemen between thieves and aggrieved property owners, charging a commission to negotiate the return of stolen goods. In a few extreme instances, thief-takers were accused of facilitating thefts so they could profit from negotiating the return of the fruits of the larcenous behaviour. Thief-takers had a deservedly gnarly reputation.

From his Bow Street office, Magistrate Sir John Fielding supervised three justices and a team of runners, men detailed to investigate crimes and arrest offenders. The

Bow Street Runners were still eligible to claim rewards, but like the justices, they also received an annual wage from the central government and were, ideally, less likely to accept bribes and other illegal pay-offs. Their focus on investigation and detection was revolutionary. Their operation in mufti occasioned fierce debate. Opponents offered a variety of arguments. To some the idea of state agents working in civilian wear, even disguises, reeked of French underhandedness and the *Brigade de la Sûreté* formed for Napoleon in 1811, by career criminal turned crime-fighter, Eugène François Vidocq. Others saw a state security apparatus that could be turned against English liberties and perverted to repressive political purposes. Many saw a permanent government force patrolling the streets as worse than the occasional excesses when the army was called in to maintain public order. Some felt petty crime should be left to local notables with traditional authority, acting as watches, sheriffs and magistrates. The Bow Street Runners were a step above thief-takers, their necessity and utility were widely acknowledged, at least among the propertied classes, but the inherent distrust of secretive agents of the government remained.

Consequently, when Home Secretary Robert Peel reorganised the system of policing London in 1829, detection and investigation were not priorities. Arguably, they were not even considerations. Peel was interested in deterrence. His 'Peelers', routinely patrolling 'beats', were to prevent crime with their regular presence, knowledge of the local underclass and overall situational awareness. They wore uniforms to enhance their visibility and deterrent effect. The uniforms were blue, not red, to clearly differentiate them from the military. There were no detectives in the new police force but the Bow Street Runners faded in importance until they were disbanded in 1839.

On June 14, 1842, the Joint Commissioners of the Metropolitan Police, barrister Richard Mayne and Lieutenant-Colonel Charles Rowan, authorised the Detective Department with an establishment of two superintendents and six sergeants dedicated to detecting the perpetrators of crimes. In large measure it was a belated response to Lord William's murder. The ensuing investigation was a shambles. It was only days after the murder and following three previous searches that stolen items were found secreted in Courvoisier's room. His lawyer suggested that the maid had placed them there to deflect the blame. Wags in the press suggested the police may have planted the evidence. Before he confessed, observers believed there were even odds that Courvoisier would not be found guilty. Officially renamed the Criminal Investigation Department in 1878, it has come to be known colloquially by the location of the Met's first headquarters, Scotland Yard. In fact and fiction, detectives and detection entered the popular consciousness in the decades around the middle of the 19th century.

Concurrently, after mid-century, newspapers became cheaper to produce and, as their cover prices dropped, circulations rose. Traditional hand presses were limited to about 200 sheets per hour, or 100, two-sheet, eight-page newspapers every 60 minutes. By 1860 a steam-powered, double-cylinder press by A B Taylor could print (and fold) 3,000 *copies* per hour, a 30-fold increase in productivity. At the same time the wholesale price of newsprint dropped considerably. Improved technology, cheap newsprint and increasing literacy were reflected in newspaper sales. Newspaper publishers could print more copies less expensively just as audiences were increasing in number. The railways increased the breadth of newspaper coverage while the telegraph expedited the spread of the news. By telegraph news of a murder in Nova Scotia would reach Toronto in hours, not days. On the opposite end of the process, a newspaper that once took days to reach Kingston could, delivered by train, be in Kingston hours after it hit the streets in Toronto. After 1850 newspapers proliferated. Even small towns sported multiple outlets. Via the train, larger metropolitan dailies, from *The Herald* to *The Globe*s (Toronto and Boston) increased the speed and the range of their circulations. As had been the case with the postal service in England, decreasing prices fostered increased circulations. This trend was plainly evident in Halifax. In 1872 the circulation of all editions of city dailies amounted to 15,500. By 1891 it had grown by 83% to 28,300. University of

Toronto historian Paul Rutherford describes this era and these developments as "an extraordinary boon to the daily" newspaper.

By the mid-1890s, a key period in Detective Power's career, the 'extraordinary boon to the daily' had led to fierce circulation wars, epitomised by the fight in New York City between Joseph Pulitzer's *New York World* and William Randolph Hearst's *New York Journal*. An English magazine in 1898 noted: "All American journalism is not 'yellow', though all strictly 'up-to-date' yellow journalism is American!" It all started over a comic strip character, the wildly popular 'Yellow Kid'. First appearing in Pulitzer's *New York World* in 1895, its artist, Richard F Outcault, was hired away by Hearst. Pulitzer responded by commissioning another artist to maintain his Yellow Kid and competing strips appeared in both papers' Sunday editions. Copyright lawsuits ensued.

The episode highlights the competition that escalated into a war and inspired yellow journalism as the two newspapers tried to outdo one another with increasingly shocking headlines and lurid reporting. The quest for sensationalism played a key role in the approaching conflict over Cuba in early 1898. Hearst dispatched famous artist Frederic Remington to Havana to illustrate his *New York Journal*'s coverage of the looming war. When Remington telegraphed that he was returning because war seemed unlikely, Hearst responded: "Please remain. You furnish the pictures and I'll furnish the war."

Days later the USS *Maine* exploded and Hearst's newspapers had their headline "The War Ship Maine was Split in Two by an Enemy's Secret Infernal Machine". Hearst had his war and Remington had his subjects, including 'Teddy' Roosevelt in his iconic 'Charge of the Rough Riders'. During the era of yellow journalism, the newspapers knew few bounds to their sensationalism as they engaged in no holds barred circulation wars.

In the 1890s newspapers were as unabashedly biased as they were sensational. In Halifax the *Herald* was openly Tory, taking on Liberals in each and every jurisdiction, federally and provincially. The *Chronicle* was equally plain as to its Grit sympathies. In terms of sensationalism, lurid headlines and column inches the *Mail* earns the crown, with the *Chronicle* offering the most staid crime coverage or, more properly, the least lurid.

For newspaper publishers the lure of crime was irresistible, as it is for today's media barons. Currently, true crime is a booming genre in the entertainment industry. Film documentaries, television dramas, podcasts and books on crimes, historical and contemporary, proliferate. Deborah Allen, vice-president of programming at Jupiter Entertainment—one of the biggest producers of true crime television in the US—told the BBC in April 2019 the industry has seen a "huge jump" in audience numbers and while "it used to be that the networks saw true crime shows as their dirty little secret," now they are front and centre of their programing schedule.

Whether these shows focus on reaffirming a verdict, highlighting a possible wrongful conviction or an unresolved cold case, they present an image of police work as deduction and forensic investigation. However, if 'it bleeds, it leads' was as true of the yellow press 125 years ago as it is today.

The Victorian public loved titillating crimes of violence and the more they violated social conventions the better. Then, as now, crime sold newspapers. Publishers knew it and obliged. While Power chased down evil-doers, Jack the Ripper's work, Lizzie Borden's axe and H H Holmes' 'Murder Castle' in Chicago competed for headlines. Readers loved being teased with obtuse references to sexual and social improprieties and explicit violence and gore. However, while the medium of the mass circulation newspaper was new, the preponderant interest in violence and death was nothing new.

It merits note that prior to the Victorian era, and throughout it, the most popular books in England, after *The Holy Bible*, were catalogues of horrors. *The Actes and Monuments*, popularly known as *Foxe's Book of Martyrs* was the next most popular volume after the Bible. First published in 1563 by John Day, the introduction stated: "Wherein are comprehended and described the great persecutions and horrible troubles that have been wrought and practised by the Romish prelates" in excruciating detail. It is a list of murders and torture from the bizarre—thrown in a river in a leather bag full of eels to the commonplace—the garrotte and stoning.

The next most popular books were collections of *The Newgate Calendar*. Subtitled *The Malefactors' Bloody Register*, they presented a monthly summary of the misdeeds and deaths of those executed at Newgate Prison, including the iconic Jack Sheppard. Compilations, known as the *Chronicles of Newgate*, detailed secular rather than religious violence, but again in horrifying detail. The massive crowds that attended public hangings also demonstrate the popular appeal of violence, criminality and death. In consideration of this growing reading public, it is hardly surprising that true crime was front and centre in the popular press.

Beside the tales of Power's derring-do, the Halifax papers regularly published stories of murder and mayhem from around the world. These were stories with no connection to Halifax and no international importance, but plenty of gory violence. On October 19, 1883, the day after Detective Power arrested Breckton and Holmes, beside that news *The Morning Herald* featured the headline on the front page "The Ashland Horror: One of the Fiends Dies on the Gallows". The crime in question involved a pair of young men beating three children to death with an axe and "they then saturated the girls' clothing with oil and set fire to the house, burning it to the ground" in rural Kentucky. This is only one example among hundreds of violent stories of crime and punishment, newsworthy for that reason alone. The more horrendous the better. Criminal violence, extending even to sexual assault and murder, was a common and constant feature of newspapers throughout the last half of the 19th century. Relevance, importance, journalistic quality, even truth, surrendered pride of place to gruesome, sensational crime and its punishment. The press and the public's obsession with violent crime persisted despite the rarity of such crimes in reality.

Journalism, a relatively new trade, had yet to develop ethical norms or standard operating procedures and the same was true of detection, to the extent that, on a slow news day during a gruesomely, noteworthy trial, journalists would simply make up the news. The production of multiple editions each day in the immediate aftermath of crimes or containing the latest testimony during trials led to sloppiness and errors. On January 29, the day after the dead body of Annie Kempton was discovered, Robert Payne, writing in the *Saint John Daily Sun* gave her age as both 15 and 17 in an article headlined succinctly and sensationally "A Horrible Murder". The young victim was, in fact, 14. Errors, fictions, suppositions presented as facts, and fantasies all proliferated in the yellow press. Fake news was alive and well to a far greater extent 150 years ago than it is today.

This was most blatantly reflected in the issue of confessions by the condemned. For the most part, the newspapers reported the condemned had confessed. Early in the century it was seen as ensuring their admission to heaven as they had 'confessed' their sin and, presumably, been divinely forgiven. Later in the century the confession took on a secular importance as it confirmed that the verdict of the court had been correct. Regardless, the tradition of confession continued, and newspapers were not above creating confessions from whole cloth if they could not gain access to the prisoner. In the case of Peter Wheeler there is every reason to believe that he never confessed and his multiple, purported confessions often, as reported, inherently contradictory, and all mutually exclusive, were the product of copy hungry newshounds and, in one noteworthy case, the product of the fertile mind of a warder and ardent Salvation Army member who had devoted his guardianship of Wheeler to converting the condemned and saving his eternal soul. During Power's tenure as a detective, fact and fiction mixed freely and frequently in the pages of newspapers as circulation wars led them to resort to sensational headlines and reportage.

Crime coverage in the newspapers of the era was influenced by the unique symbiosis that developed between journalists and detectives—they needed each other. Detective Power needed the *Halifax Herald*, and the *Halifax Herald*, and every other newspaper in Nova Scotia, needed Nic Power. Power provided the press with quotes and copy and the press provided Power with a podium that, through repetition, transubstantiated his theories into facts.

The players in the courts were fully aware of the weight

the newspapers carried. In one of the cases in which Power figured, defence counsel greeted the prosecution's introduction of a surprise witness with the argument "it is done, I daresay, for newspaper effect because the government realizes its case is weak, and this effort was made for the purpose of prejudicing the case in the newspapers". In another instance, a news report on a coroner's inquest did not transcribe witness testimony because, as it explained, the witness's testimony had already been published the day before following an interview by a journalist.

In terms of police procedure, along with detection, forensic science began to figure in investigations. Some proved dead ends such as phrenology, while others were decades in the future, including ballistics or DNA analysis. However, scientific methods were increasingly applied to criminal detection in the last half of the 19th century. Then, as now, both the prosecution and the defence could often find 'experts' to support their versions of events. These experts frequently disagreed in a vituperative, personal manner. Juries, scientifically ill-informed, often dismissed all the contradictory 'scientific' testimony, and turned to common sense, as uncommon and incorrect as it often is, when rendering a verdict. At other times juries averred, awed by the weight of scientific 'fact'. In the late Victorian era forensic science was making its way into the courtroom but its techniques were rudimentary and its evidence often questioned.

Cultural trends, namely the invention of murder and the ascension of the 'scientific detective', encountering the brash, bold and egotistical Detective Power would ultimately result in a cyclone that destroyed more than one life. An obsession with violent death, murder and mayhem permeated late Victorian culture and was typified by the sensational headlines and endless inches of copy devoted to gory descriptions of ghastly crimes no matter how obscure and irrelevant their setting. Did a Haligonian really *need* to know about an incestuous preacher in Paducah, Kentucky, or an infant's abduction in Dubuque, Iowa? This obsession had a flipside that rendered impotent the threat of violent death, reducing it to mere titillation, and that was the detective. Be it Nic Power or Sherlock Holmes, real or imagined, near or far, equilibrium and stability was sustained and the threat disarmed by the heroic detective's solution of the mystery. The public, obsessed with murder and mayhem, desperately wanted a superhero in the person of a scientific detective; the press was willing to provide one; and Detective Nicolas Power was pleased to play the role. For the other members of the cast the results can only be described as mixed.

Ironically, this discussion started with a novel, *Jack Sheppard*, and it is bookended by a novel published in 1914, seven years after our bad detective had retired. *The After House: A Story of Love, Mystery and a Private Yacht* by popular novelist Mary Roberts Rinehart was loosely, very loosely, based on a multiple murder investigation Power played a key role in. Recognising her readers' sensibilities, the author transfigured a Harvard dropout into the hero and wrote out the first mate, a mere seaman of indeterminate origins, who was the real hero. In this case Power's bungled interrogation would result in the US Supreme Court ordering a retrial, which still resulted in a wrongful conviction, but not a capital sentence. *The After House* became a favourite of an ex-President who took his concerns to the President, who eventually pardoned the wrongly convicted man. Anecdotes and events surrounding *Jack Sheppard*'s publication in 1839, and those following the publication of *The Aft House* 75 years later capture the links between fact and fiction, fantasy and reality that characterised the public, the press and Power during his detecting career. It was in this fertile environment that a bad detective, Nicholas Power, was transformed into a 'super sleuth'. Novels, theatre, journalism and the criminal justice system all contributed to the emergence of detection and the detective as cultural memes. It was all fertile ground for an egotistical detective like Power to sow his seeds of suspicion and see them grow into truths and legal judgements.

CHAPTER FOUR

Saving the Prince Revisited

IN RECOGNITION of the centenary of the Declaration of Independence, the Centennial International Exhibition of 1876, the first official World's Fair held in the US, opened in Philadelphia, Pennsylvania on Wednesday, May 10. The Japanese Bazaar comprised a main pavilion surrounded by an authentic garden including a teahouse, cherry trees and an innocent-looking vine, introduced to North America for the first time, known as kudzu. In Japan it is frequently grown on trellises to provide shade. Its remarkable growth rate, one foot per day and as much as 60 feet per growing season, marks it apart from any other plant.

It also gave it immense appeal to railway builders at a time when construction was booming, with both Canada and the US racing to complete transcontinental railways. Trains cannot tolerate steep grades. Consequently, their designers are constantly struggling to level the railbed. Prominent features must be cut down and watercourses and ravines must be bridged or filled with embankments. In North America the largest of the latter is known as 'The Big Fill'. To avoid blasting an 800-foot tunnel through the Promontory Mountains, the surveyors of the Central Pacific Railroad decided to construct an embankment, not a bridge, across the 500-foot Spring Creek ravine. Ultimately, the railways advancing from the Pacific and Atlantic coasts would be linked with the 'Golden Spike' at the adjacent hamlet of Promontory, Utah.

Erosion presents a constant threat to these earthen structures and the roots of plants provide an inexpensive antidote. Kudzu's rapid growth made it ideal for the purpose and it was widely adopted after 1876. Across the US the railroads planted millions of kudzu. It has since become an incredibly destructive, invasive species with the moniker 'the plant that ate the South'. It has been known to climb utility poles and lines, its weight pulling them down, and swallow tobacco kilns and farm machinery. At the time, unintended consequences unforeseen, it became essential to filling declivities in the railbed.

While kudzu facilitated embankment construction and maintenance, dynamite was the weapon of choice for blasting out cuts after it was developed and its production commercialised by Alfred Nobel, commencing in 1867. Needless to add, mining operations, both open pit and subterranean, also saw the immense potential of dynamite. Nova Scotia had witnessed a minor mining boom following the discovery of gold in 1858. After two decades the rush slowed until the proliferation of dynamite allowed deeper diggings and reignited the fever in the late 1870s. In Halifax, F D Corbett & Co, at 135 Lower Water Street, were the sole agents of Nobel's Explosive Company. They advertised in the local newspapers regularly. Under the headline "Important to Miners" they offered dynamite "This GENUINE and RELIABLE article, the Most Powerful and Economical Explosive… On the most favourable terms." They also stocked "Treble Charge Detonators, Fuse, Warming Pans, and other requisites at lowest rates." As bizarre as it may seem, while dynamite was hardly commonplace, its possession and use were in no way as carefully regulated as they are today. Like a host of commonplace articles, it could be legally transported across the Canada-US border by anyone, provided it was declared and federal excise taxes and duties were paid.

Itinerant miners were frequently expected to supply their own tools and supplies, including dynamite. Gold mining was largely organised under the tribute system in Nova Scotia. The claim was usually owned by an investor, a nascent capitalist from the provincial elite who would not actually work it. He would lease it to miners, known as tributers, who would pay their lease with a share of the gold they extracted. Depending on one's perspective, the tributers were independent contractors like gig workers today or sharecroppers like recently freed slaves in the Jim Crow south. In either case, small-scale tributers from away had good reason to carry their own dynamite. Arriving in the Nova Scotia gold fields from the US local merchants would have charged them top dollar for poor quality, adulterated dynamite. Simply put, to get the biggest bang for their buck, itinerant miners were strictly BYOD—bring your own dynamite.

This lack of legislation and restrictions covering dynamite, and its proliferation coupled with its explosive potential, led it to become something of a cultural phenomenon, a late-Victorian meme. Its stability and safety, relative to nitroglycerine, encouraged a casual attitude toward dynamite that would seem remarkable today. Beyond engineering and advertising, it was referenced constantly in the press. *The Morning Herald* of Thursday, May 8, 1884 is illustrative. A dozen column inches of the front page detail an alleged plot to destroy the Ontorio legislature in Toronto with dynamite. More specifically, proudly and loudly Tory, the *Herald* criticised Oliver Mowat's provincial Liberal government's attempts to make political hay of the discovery. Subsequently, the *Herald* would have to defend itself against the Liberal *Chronicle*'s slurs that it was treating dynamite too 'flippantly'. When Power convinced himself he was amid a Fenian plot he was preaching to the choir. Fenians and dynamite were on everyone's lips and the scribes gleefully fanned the flames.

On the opposite, outer edge of the same front page, May 8, 1884, is a small article headlined: "The Dynamiters Sentenced". It details the outcome of the only case of dynamite smuggling prosecuted in Halifax that year. The two perpetrators were found guilty and sentenced to six months in prison. No account was taken of their six months in pre-trial custody. *The Morning Herald* opined recently appointed Supreme Court Justice John David Sparrow Thompson had settled on "probably a lighter sentence than the public at large were expecting". A future Prime Minister of Canada, the judge was expected to impose a harsher sentence because the parties in question were none other than James Holmes and William Breckton, accused by Detective Power of being Fenian assassins.

The disposition of the case clearly indicates that the justice system rejected Detective Power's fantastic narrative. Both the Crown Prosecutor and Judge Thompson explicitly dismissed Power's claim that the arrest had short-circuited an assassination that would have had profound diplomatic and political aftershocks. The prosecutor chose to lay only minor charges despite the newspaper hysteria surrounding the arrest. Justice Thompson reinforced the trivial nature of the offence with a notably short sentence. The final disposition of the case clearly indicates that the justice system categorically rejected

Power's theory that the two men were Fenian terrorists, intent on disposing of the Prince and his crewmates. The entire theory was a figment of Power's imagination. It was a fantasy concocted by the detective, into which the facts were made, or made up, to fit. Conveniently, it played to the paranoia and fevered atmosphere around Fenians long present in Canadian memory, and recently inflamed by the bombing campaign in the British Isles. Power's theory was amplified by the sensational headlines and coverage that the incident garnered. His theory had become accepted fact only days after the arrest, long before the accused had benefit of a judge and jury.

The terrifying 'diving skirt', a key element of the conspiracy, disappeared from the prosecution, if it ever existed in the first place. Lynea Wilson, Assistant Curator of the History of Diving Museum in Islamorada, Florida was unable to offer any insight into such a 'swimming suit'. In purely practical terms it seems implausible that such a suit could have been constructed in the 1880s. Given the state of the rubber and fabric industries in the 1880s it is virtually impossible that proper seals could have been constructed that would have maintained pressure and floatation. The incriminating 'diving' suit may never have existed, like the plot itself. Or with Power's penchant for hyperbole, what he initially told the newspapers was a diving skirt may have simply been a pair of hip waders. Hip waders had only been marketed for a few decades and were relatively uncommon before 1912, when aniline accelerated vulcanisation dramatically reduced the cost of rubber products. While this theory is merely speculation, the simple fact of the matter is that the 'diving skirt' that figured so highly in the initial newspaper reports played no role in the trial.

No record of the court proceedings was preserved due to the minor nature of the charges actually laid against the pair. However, the proof is in the pudding or, in this case, the sentence. As noted earlier, Breckton and Holmes were sentenced to six months in prison in addition to the six months they had already spent incarcerated. In total they would spend approximately one year in Rockhead, the city prison, at the corner of Leeds and Gottingen streets.

However, surely if they were suspected of attempting to kill a member of the royal family they would have been charged with a more significant offence? If the evidence supported Power's claim that the Prince was the target, they could have been charged with conspiracy to commit murder, attempted murder, even treason. That the charges were reduced to simply smuggling dynamite speaks volumes. Essentially, the justice system was registering its belief that Breckton and Holmes were not Fenian assassins. Their landlord's testimony, "they said they were going to the gold fields", was no alibi. It was the simple, but inconvenient truth.

Again, consider the sentence. If the prosecution did not have the evidence to prefer a more serious charge than smuggling dynamite it could still have registered its opprobrium at sentencing. Suspected of malevolent plans for murder, the court could have acknowledged its concerns with a long sentence. It did not. The court and Justice John Sparrow David Thompson gave the pair a slap on the wrist. Clearly, the prosecution, the judge and the court, the entire justice system, gave no credence to Power's theory that the pair were Fenian assassins.

The heinous plot was fiction. Power's elaborate narrative, purportedly a brilliant insight into the machinations of Irish nationalist extremists, was a flight of fancy. The blaring headlines and gory details broadcast by the yellow press was much ado about nothing. Sam Slick, the Yankee pedlar *cum* con man protagonist of Nova Scotian Thomas Haliburton's 1840 novel *The Clockmaker* summed it all up if we simply substitute 'Fenians' for 'her timper': "All that talk about her timper was made out of whole cloth, and got up a-purpose… What a fib!... It's all made out of whole cloth." Like a conjurer pulling a rabbit out of a top hat, Power pulled a royal assassination plot out of the Parker House hotel. It was a fabrication. In modern terms, the Fenian plot to dynamite the *Canada* was as real as the assertion that Saddam Hussein had massive stockpiles of weapons of mass destruction. Power's conspiracy was a pants on fire lie.

None of the Halifax newspapers offered any explanations for their previous sensational coverage. Retractions were unheard of in the heat of yellow journalism's circulation wars. The *Herald*'s brief acknowledgement of a 'lighter sentence than the public at large were expecting' was a step above the *Chronicle*. Despite extensive research in the municipal and provincial archives, and the Halifax Central Library local history collection, no evidence of the *Chronicle* mentioning their conviction or sentencing could be found. In the face of their hysterical coverage of the initial arrests and the claims of terrorist intentions and international implications, the Halifax newspapers choose barely a whisper as a response to their earlier hyperbole. All that remained, it seems, was the strongly-held memory that the headlines had touted Power's spectacular arrest of Fenian bombers and that was not a false memory. The problem was that the remembered headlines were wrong.

In October 1883 there was a great hue and cry over Fenian perfidy and threats against Halifax, shipping and the Royal Navy. The specific assassination theory originated with Detective Nicholas Power alone. This singular narrative was then amplified and broadcast widely by the newspapers. Whether the newspapers collaborated with Power or were merely compliant is open to interpretation. It is also moot. The public at the time believed that Detective Power had saved the Prince's life, despite the fact that it had never been threatened, because the newspapers had broadcast as fact Power's narrative speculation. The newspapers then under-reported the actual disposition of the case and declined to publish retractions or corrections. The public may have been confused by misinformation but the justice system—judges, lawyers, clerks—and the journalists knew that the truth of the matter was that there was no murderous conspiracy.

Their silence raises a troubling question. Why did they not 'out' Power and proclaim that Power's grandiose vision of the implications of his arrest was a lie? This question will linger throughout Power's career. Did Power's confidence fool them and his reputation overpower them? During the era's newspaper wars were journalists more concerned with effect than fact, favouring sensation over accuracy? Were the journalists complicit in Power's myth-making? Were they collaborators with Power? Did they conspire with Power? Or were they simply slipshod, lapping up his pronouncements to fill the reading public's insatiable demand for murder and mayhem? These are all issues that arise repeatedly throughout Power's career.

Stranger still, the newspapers (and more modern media such as the Internet) have continued to sustain the myth for almost 150 years. Articles noting his promotion to chief in 1906, upon his retirement 18 months later, his obituaries in 1938, and periodic features all remarked on his erudition in preventing the Prince's death. Constant repetition made the myth real, so real that it was repeated in an extensive feature about Power published in the *Chronicle-Herald* weekly magazine as recently as 2010. Since October 1883 the story that Detective Power foiled a Fenian bombing and saved the Prince, as well as the captain and crew of the *Canada*, has developed a life of its own and become accepted as fact. It is untrue. It is a myth. It is a lie that Nic Power knew was a lie, yet still chose to actively and persistently repeat. In blunter terms, Nic Power was a liar.

The bad detective's career, his reputation for thorough investigations turning up unlikely evidence that led him, brilliantly, to detect the guilty party, was a Paul Bunyan-like tall tale. More importantly, his public persona, courtesy of a willingly gullible media, was based on nothing but hype. Power's foundation myth, the basis of his eminence as a detective, was proven to be false shortly after it was manufactured by the press. Noteworthy, this is not a case of hindsight being 20-20. That was the opinion at the time. Not possibly ill-informed popular opinion, but the reasoned decision of one of the generation's leading legal minds. One could argue no amount of self-confidence and braggadocio can make fiction fact. But that is exactly what has occurred here. A conspiracy theory proven to be a non-existent fiction has written itself into the historical record by virtue of its proponent's persistence and constant repetition—his tenacity.

Power's fantasies almost came close to being prescient in December 1884 when three men were caught in a small craft trying to attach a bomb to one of the arches of London Bridge. Wrong continent and wrong craft, but the only incident close to Power's nightmarish visions. It would be almost a century before the Irish

Republican Army succeeded in an aquatic attack. On August 27, 1979 a 23kg bomb exploded on a wooden fishing boat off the western coast of the Republic of Ireland, killing Lord Louis Mountbatten and others aboard his yacht *Shadow V*. Despite Power's extravagant theory and the hubbub raised by the newspapers, the verdict of the courts, and of history, must be that there was no plot and, by definition, no plot foiled. Detective Power did not save the future king. He did not prevent a Fenian bombing because there was no Fenian plot. It never happened.

Despite its manifest untruth, and the newspapers' awareness of the falsehood, the episode became Power's foundation myth. A foundation myth provides a basis and justification for a set of beliefs, cultural system, nation or other group. Romulus and Remus, twin brothers and founders of Rome, being suckled by a *lupa* (she-wolf), is an example of a political or national foundation myth. The Christian version of the life of Jesus Christ, from immaculate conception through betrayal and crucifixion to ascension, provides an example of a religious foundation myth. Manifestly untrue foundation myths become cultural touchstones and justification for a wider set of beliefs, norms and values.

Power's foundation myth was the fantastic story that his investigative prowess saved the life of the young Prince. The eminence of the target, the potential consequences of a successful attack, established the importance of detection and detectives (particularly the gifted soul that was Power). It stood as evidence of his skill as a detective and, as such, proof of the accuracy of his later reconstructions of crimes and identification of perpetrators. Subsequently, memories of this coup would be repeated to add weight to Power's later investigative conclusions. This tendency reached its peak shortly after he was appointed Chief of the Halifax Police Department on January 1, 1906. Despite the promotion he was dispatched by the provincial Attorney General to investigate the suspicious death of Anton Stetka, a coal miner, his wife and two young children on Cape Breton island. They were found dead in the charred remains of their home. The coroner's inquest was inconclusive. A likely suspect had both motive and opportunity. Nonetheless, shortly after arriving on the scene, Power announced that no crime had been committed. His justification for his conclusion was not evidence, it was his reputation. At the time he explained to *The Glace Bay Gazette*: "I have had some experience in investigating suspicious fires and their causes, and I have more than once come to a correct solution on the conclusion of matters of this kind." In plainer English, Power asserted that events unfolded the way he said they did because he said they did. Solipsism at its finest. Power's overwhelming influence, spawned by his apparent omniscience and extraordinary erudition, grew out of the initial newspaper reportage of his narrative of a Fenian plot. That imaginary triumph added weight to any of his pronouncements, as he was the 'Man who saved the Prince."

This seminal event in Power's public career reveals a great deal about Power's methods. He was willing to extrapolate from the facts to create a sensational, (aka front page-worthy) situation—miners with dynamite become Fenians with assassination on their minds. Avoiding hyperbole was not one of Power's strong suits. He loved to blow his own horn, and did so early and often. One can only laugh when reading his obituary: "This reporter never tired of sitting in his modest, comfortable home on Dresden Row and listening to yarns of the days when he wore 'the blue'. Not that he would willingly reminisce. For 'Nick' Power was a modest man." Falser words have never been spoken.

He was willing to speak openly and often to correspondents, to the extent that Power announced his *ad hoc* verdict before the powers that be ruled *de jure*. He tried cases in the court of public opinion, via the newspapers, before the accused had a chance to stand before a jury of his peers. In modern terms, Power was not only an investigator, he was an influencer. He used the newspapers to promote his product—his narrative of a crime—the way influencers today use Twitter and Instagram. He rushed to judgement, obstinately unwilling to consider alternatives, and then aggressively lobbied for his version of events with the result that his narrative won in the court of public opinion before the justice system had a chance to rule.

It bears repeating that the newshounds aided and abetted Power every step of the way. They willingly and uncritically published his speculation as fact. Power was a media darling. The journalists knew he was always good for a quote and would often expostulate at length. They also knew that their readers loved stories of bloody mayhem. Alongside the news stories detailing Power's investigations of Nova Scotian murders appear bizarre, ghastly news stories from obscure corners of the globe, noteworthy only for their violence and horror. "Corpse in His Cellar. Petrified Head and Trunk of a Girl—He Died While Perfecting Process" is merely typical. 'If it bleeds it leads' ruled the yellow journalism of Power's era, and the crimes he investigated usually bled.

Consequently, the newspapers reported on them at length, enabled by Power. Each party facilitated the other. Power would rush to judgement quickly and the media would then broadcast his sensational claims to the public as fact. The two, Power and the newshounds, shared a symbiotic relationship. Together they hyped horrific violence and bathetic tragedy, titillating readers while they fostered fear and public hysteria. In the race to increase readership they flocked to the scenes of major crimes; crime scenes regularly presided over by Detective Power.

Despite the minor charges that Breckton and Holmes were eventually convicted of, the case counts as the most important in Power's policing career. It was his first major case following his promotion to the rank of detective. Second, his supposed unravelling of this non-existent plot remained true in the public mind, so true that it became his foundation myth—both evidence of, and justification for, his monumental detection skills. Detective Nic Power could foresee future events. He could take seemingly unconnected pieces of evidence, overlooked or dismissed by others, and construct a chain of evidence that revealed crimes and their perpetrators. These skills made him Canada's Sherlock Holmes.

The problem, of course, is that Detective Power had done nothing of the kind. He had created a conspiracy out of whole cloth. There was, in fact, nothing there. But there were consequences. The incident cemented Detective Power's image of infallibility in the popular press and the public mind and others, many others, would pay dearly to preserve that simulacrum. In this case, the long-forgotten Holmes and Breckton whiled away a year of their lives in Rockwood Prison because Nic Power was full of himself, and the press and public had lapped it up. In future others would pay a far greater price as a result of Power's overblown image.

Forensic anthropologist Debra Komar has extensively researched one specific case, that of Peter Wheeler, which Detective Power took the lead in. In an interview she asserted: "Nic Power could never admit he was wrong, and he was always wrong." The latter claim is hyperbole, Detective Power was only often wrong.

Even bad detectives occasionally get it right. It is true, however, that he could never admit he was wrong. Like a dog with a bone, once he had a suspect, he hung on. Right or wrong, he was tenacious. Unfortunately, he was frequently doggedly wrong.

CHAPTER FIVE

The First Fifty (1843-1893)

DURING ITS early years, sporadic raids and ongoing guerrilla warfare dictated the layout of Halifax. Initial development focused on the connection between Citadel Hill and the waterfront. The area was enclosed by wooden palisades running from the fort to the port. Schmidt's Ville, 800m south of Citadel Hill, was Halifax's first development outside the wire: its first suburb. Established in 1830, now a historic district, it is known today as Schmidtville.

In 1781 James Pedley purchased 12 acres of land south of Citadel Hill. His daughter Elizabeth inherited the property upon his death in 1807. Elizabeth was married to Captain Christian Wilhelm Schmidt of King George III's Royal Foreign Artillery. In 1830, two years after his death, Elizabeth subdivided Pedley's fields into 79 building lots. By 1837 the area was largely developed extending south from Spring Garden Road to Holy Cross Cemetery, between Dresden Row and Queen Street.

Nic Power was conceived, born and died in Schmidt's Ville. He lived most of his life in these dozen blocks, residing at the southwest corner of Birmingham and Clyde for much of his time wearing 'the blue' and passing away at his daughter's home near the corner of Dresden Row and Spring Garden Road 75 years later. He was born on Sunday, June 11, 1843. His father, Patrick, was a mechanic and his mother's maiden name had been Bridget Murphy. Considering his lifelong residence in Schmidt's Ville it is not unreasonable to suggest that he was born there. A second boy, John, joined the family in September, 1845.

Very little is known of young Nic's childhood and education. The Halifax Grammar School, then located at the northwest corner of Barrington and Sackville streets, would have provided his early education. The tuition of $20 annually was presumably affordable as his father was some type of craftsman or skilled tradesman (the contemporary definition of the job description mechanic). His career trajectory indicates that his literacy and numeracy were well above average. Regardless, Power offered little about his life before his entry into the Royal Navy.

He had spent four years in the Navy, enlisting in 1860. He served as a butcher's boy on the complement of

HMS *Nile*, a Rodney-class, two-deck 90-gun second rate, designed for the Royal Navy by Sir Robert Seppings. Carrying the flag of Rear Admiral Alexander Milne, the Commander-in-Chief, North America and West Indies Station, *Nile* operated from Bermuda and Halifax. Signifying resolution of the conflicts between Britain and the US during the first years of the US Civil War, *Nile* made a ceremonial visit to New York City in September 1863.

Whether Power was actually aboard ship on its visit to New York City is unknown. At the time there were various grades of boy seamen in the Royal Navy. Domestic staff on flagships, graded as Boy 3rd Class frequently did not live aboard. Power may very well have remained at home with his parents while labouring at the butcher's behest when she was in port. On duty he would have been responsible for everything and anything from scrubbing pots to running errands ashore. Giving credit where credit is due, Power, who rarely let pass a chance to hyperbolise, never laid claim to combat experience or naval heroics during his brief tenure as a Jack Tar.

The Halifax municipal government authorised the amalgamation of the watches and the creation of the Halifax Police Department under Marshall Garrett Cotter in October 1864. Within a month, on Wednesday, November 16, 1864, the new department hired the strapping young naval veteran. When novice Constable Nicholas Power donned 'the blue' he was a 21-year-old, newly married and with a child on the way. With the end of his naval service in sight, on Tuesday, April 26, 1864 he married Mary Jane Sheehan, a few years his junior, at St Mary's Basilica Cathedral. Their first child, Alice, would arrive in July 1865. Tragically, she would die in 1886. Mary Jane would bear another 10 children, seven surviving into adulthood.

In 1870 his growing family lived at 13 Grafton Street, a few blocks north of Schmidt's Ville. Later in the decade he returned to Schmidt's Ville, renting a flat at Birmingham and Clyde streets (currently 1350-60 Birmingham Street). Interestingly, in 1861 the first set of quadruplets in Nova Scotia, all boys, had been born in the building, when shoemaker John Ryan's wife gave birth. Ironically, considering the prominence of alcohol in both policing and disciplining the guardians, Power's landlord was apparently in the liquor business, and the storefront facing the intersection (currently Nova Grocery—'the convenience that has everything at reasonable prices') probably sold alcohol.

Nicholas Power was a Roman Catholic of Irish descent. A member of the Catholic Mutual Benefit Society, he worshipped at St Mary's Basilica Cathedral on the northwest corner of Barrington and Spring Garden Road. Nova Scotia ironstone with a sandstone facade, construction commenced in 1820. Only the third stone building in Halifax, its outsized roof was framed by shipwrights familiar with complex curves and distributing loads because there were no other qualified carpenters or builders in the colony. Whether Nic had taken the pledge or was an occasional drinker is unknown. It is known, and noteworthy, that over the 43 years of his career, in an era when police personnel were regularly drunk on duty, Nic never faced those accusations. On this issue he seems to have been a model policeman.

On June 5, 1893, after seven years as a widow, Nic married again. His bride, Alice Callaghan, a dozen years younger than Nic, had been born in Prince Edward Island of Irish Roman Catholic descent about 1857. Through more than 40 years of marriage they had no children. She died on January 22, 1934. Nic, 91 at the time, then moved in with his daughter Lillian, at 119 Dresden Row, near Spring Garden Road. It was there, in Schmidtville, that he died on Sunday, October 2, 1938 at the ripe old age of 95.

Hired on as a constable, Nic Power's first few years in the department seem to have passed in obscurity. No disciplinary issues brought him to the attention of the police committee. A mere constable, he does not appear to have garnered newspaper attention. He would have spent his time on duty engaged in the time-honoured pursuits of Halifax's guardians, in the Upper Streets among familiar recidivists, arresting drunks, bootleggers, prostitutes and gamblers.

His first big break occurred before he was promoted to sergeant in 1873 and may have led to his promotion. John E Albro, a wealthy Halifax merchant, resided at

89 Morris Street. He was Halifax royalty, his grandfather, also named John, was one of the earliest settlers in Nova Scotia, arriving from Rhode Island. By 1800 John the elder was a merchant eventually specialising in hardware and ship chandlery. A vestryman at St Paul's Church and Lieutenant-Colonel of the 4th Regiment of Halifax militia, he was involved in the establishment of everything from the Fire Insurance Association of Halifax to the Halifax Steamship Company. Eventually, the patriarch's wealth passed on to his children and grandchildren.

In 1870 John E, in partnership with Joseph Weir, operated Albro Son & Co, a ship chandlery offering everything from anvils and anchors to whip thongs and whiting. His younger brother Edward operated a similar establishment. John E had a massive, five storefront outlet on Hollis Street and a satellite location on Duke Street. John E was also the victim of a burglary. Of a Sunday evening, with his wife, and two servant girls in tow, they had all attended church. Upon their return it was discovered that jewellery and silver plate to a value of approximately $1,000 (a small fortune at the time; that such a windfall was available speaks to John E's wealth).

The Halifax police, including Constable Power, were summoned. It was quickly deduced that the thieves had entered by the front door, making their escape through the rear door and over a fence. Otherwise, there seemed to be no evidence as to the culprits. Power, however, noticed a candle stub, an unusual candle stub, that he suspected the thieves had used. He pocketed the candle stub and the next day he took it to various chandlers and hardware merchants. At the head of Market Wharf, at Thomas Lahey's shop, he hit gold. Lahey was the only importer of the candles, they had recently arrived and he had only sold one lot, to the Royal Artillery canteen.

Further investigation revealed that the Albro's servant girls were being courted by military men, artillerymen to be specific. They confessed, implicating a third, and the trio were convicted. Most of the stolen goods were eventually recovered, with a fiscal reward returned to the department. Constable Nic Power's reputation as a 'thief-taker' was established, and established in all the right places. The newspapers were lavish in their praise, introducing the eagle-eyed constable to the public. This was Nic Power's first flirtation with public attention. It can be assumed both that he enjoyed it and he appreciated its value to his career prospects because he would assiduously cultivate the newshawks throughout his career.

On an entirely different level, Constable Power's name became known to the Southside bluebloods that ran the province. Politicians and power brokers, merchants and property owners, the Halifax elite, would now have known Nic Power's name, and that he was an up-and-comer, someone to keep an eye on. After the Albro case Constable Nic Power looked like a good cop—erudite, persistent and tenacious. Subsequently, on July 15, 1871 Constable Power was promoted to the rank of sergeant.

In April 1873, Power was sent to the Peggy's Cove area 10 miles southwest of Halifax. Today, its famous lighthouse is one of the most photographed locations in the world. Then, an American highwayman was terrorising the St Margaret's Bay Road from Halifax. Recalling the incident, *The Herald* noted: "Without any newspaper talk that officer [Detective Power] and his assistants speedily captured the highwayman." Nic Power knew how to keep his name in the news.

His reputation would survive a black eye on the entire department that Power played a role in. On August 1, 1876 P T Barnum's circus arrived in town. They marched into town from the north end Richmond station, right past the Bank of Nova Scotia, repository of the provincial treasury, at 166 Hollis Street. The bank staff were unable to resist the parading pachyderms and piled onto the street, leaving only the charwoman in the bank. The *Herald* later reported: "A man of decent appearance asked the janitor's wife if he might go to the basement to look for an article lost through the grating." She complied and he, apparently, helped himself to the tin box holding the provincial treasury—a sum variously estimated as between $22,000 and $31,000. The tin box, empty except for a single cheque and a few cents, was later recovered in a shed on the South End wharf. Power, on the case, quickly arrested two Americans, Hampton and Watson, dining in the French

House hotel, across from the train station. He accused them of having hidden the loot on the train and preparing to flee. When nothing was found secreted on the train, he insisted that was too obvious, the money was hidden in the city, to be retrieved later. Eventually, no charges were brought forward against the hapless diners and they were released. Other suspects were also investigated but no one was ever charged and the case remained unsolved, despite the hurried return to England of a senior bank employee only days after the theft.

Power was not responsible for this case not being solved or, if he was, it was only indirectly. His immediate accusations may have tempered the investigation of other possible suspects. Thankfully, no innocents were mistakenly convicted. Remarkably, the Bank of Nova Scotia survived Forman's deceit and the circus caper, remaining one of Canada's 'Big Six' banks today. Most importantly, this incident demonstrates that at this stage in his career, admittedly early, Power was far from infallible and, as had been the case with Breckton and Holmes, an early arrest by Power was in no way the same as a conviction in the courts.

The hasty departure of the employee and the fruitless investigation is not entirely surprising. The Halifax elite has always demonstrated a tendency to close in on itself, avoiding public scandal, for private solutions. This was not the first time this was evident. In 1857 the government powder magazine exploded. While no one was killed, the damage and loss of inventory was severe. The magazine's elderly attendant was chronically ill and off the job. The only key was held by Alexander Keith. Not Alexander Keith the world-renowned brewer, but rather his young nephew, Alexander 'Sandy' Keith. The latter's life would end when another explosion he engineered killed dozens in Germany and he committed suicide. However, in 1857 no one in Halifax was willing to accuse the elder Alexander Keith's nephew of such a crime and, following an official inquiry, the explosion was attributed to improper storage on the part of the absent attendant.

A similar tendency to avoid public scandal was evident in the case of James Forman, first cashier (equivalent to the chief operating officer today) and founding director of the Bank of Nova Scotia. As Forman approached 40 years of service, in August 1870, it was discovered he had steadily and stealthily embezzled $315,000 over a quarter of a century. The bank's other directors stayed silent and the Halifax elite closed ranks. Forman signed over Thorndean, his three-storey Georgian residence in the South End and all its contents to be auctioned. Suspiciously, it seems to have been purchased at a discount by the selfsame bank's president, John S Maclean. Bottom-line, Forman repaid $180,000 and the bank ate the loss of $135,000. More notable, Forman was never charged with a crime and allowed to return to England, where he promptly died. Meanwhile, the *Chronicle* argued that the directors had been negligent, lamenting "there is no way to punish the criminally careless directors." The courts were below the bluebloods and they did not air their dirty laundry in public.

Most relevantly, this early bank job is revelatory of a theme in Power's career. Power was a bloodhound. He was a natural born hunter. He loved tracking prey. Once he had his sights on a target, he was tenacious in his pursuit. His greatest successes involved tracking quarry, particularly thieves and fraudsters, which he did, with notable success, all over North America (the bank job being a notable exception to that skill). Power's single-mindedness was often an asset. His laser-like focus, when he was mistaken, was his greatest weakness, blinding him to alternative narratives and suspects.

In 1882, Halifax Police Department detective William Hutt died. Unsurprisingly, he was succeeded by the sergeant who had been with the department since its inception and demonstrated a talent for detection. On November 18, 1882 Sergeant Nicholas Power dropped 'the blue' and began serving in civvies, courtesy of the taxpayer, as the department's second detective. He took on the role as an Irish nationalist bombing campaign was tearing England apart. An urgent telegram would arrive only months after he took office from the federal government's secret sources warning of a Fenian plot against shipping into and out of the port. In this fevered atmosphere freshman Detective Nicolas Power, with the willing compliance of the newspapers, manufactured a Fenian plot to bomb the *Canada* and kill the Prince. Despite the plot being fantasy, a product of Power's imagination and the alleged plotters eventually being convicted only of smuggling dynamite for use in their mining efforts, the public were left with a wildly different impression.

Power's initial, unjustified and megalomaniacal claim to having prevented an explosive tragedy, survived. Broadcast internationally by telegraph, the news was published widely, drawing more attention to, and praise for, Detective Power. Virtually no newspaper attention was paid to the fact that the court rejected the idea of a nefarious plot, sentencing the pair to a pedestrian six months in Rockwood Prison. Indeed, and truly strangely, the court's decision that there was no Fenian plot afoot was seemingly simply ignored by the press and the public.

Detective Nic Power's foundation myth was firmly established and persistent. It had legs. Detective Power, the big, burly, barely 40-year-old detective, was the 'Man who saved the Prince', notwithstanding the absolute, undeniable untruth of the claim. His foundation was rotten, he was a bad detective from his roots. A couple of innocents swept up in a brief maelstrom was all the Fenian hysteria amounted to. Regardless, Power lied and continued to lie about the incident for the next 55 years. He was a bad detective at his core and from the get-go. His reputation predicated on a falsehood, he can hardly be held up as a model of rectitude and integrity. Despite his undeserved reputation for erudition and the cash value his recovery of stolen goods returned, by the end of the 1880s Detective Power was confronting troubled waters. His performance and his value to the community were about to both come under fire.

Throughout more than four decades of service, prior to assuming the chief's role and becoming a member of the Police Commission, Power was largely absent from the endless disciplinary deliberations of the Police Committee and its successor the Police Commission. Never did he face the apparently commonplace charges related to intoxication and both of his appearances in the minutes were exceptional. The most significant, occupying the committee for the entire summer of 1889, and pages of unusually loquacious documentation, raised questions about Power's methods.

In the spring of 1889, an investigation took Power to Boston. Upon its successful conclusion and his return to Halifax he submitted his expenses to the committee. They complained that a hotel bill, at four dollars a night for a week, was exorbitant. They categorically refused to reimburse another $35 of the amount Power had submitted. Power claimed the $35 for three disbursements, two of $10 each to a pair of informants and a third payment of $15 to a private detective in Boston. The committee objected because the trio were unnamed, and Power refused to identify them. Eventually, the matter was resolved when Power met privately with the chairman of the police committee and offered an *in camera* explanation and, perhaps, their names. While their discussions are unknowable, the chairman's curiosity was sufficiently assuaged that he felt comfortable assuring the committee the payments had been legitimate. Power's brief suspension was lifted and he returned to duty, but his motives merit investigation.

Power may have been protecting the informants, possibly underworld figures themselves, however it is more difficult to explain his refusal to name the private dick. One might be tempted to suggest that Power, as many do, simply padded his expense account. This seems highly unlikely given his otherwise unblemished disciplinary record. In small, straightforward matters, those of 'cash register' honesty, Nic Power was a man of considerable rectitude, arguably even self-righteous. The bad detective's vague association with truth emerged only in Dr Goebbels' 'big lie'. There is also a more nuanced explanation borne out by corroborating evidence. Detective Power was expressing his gargantuan ego by defending his conduct and his turf. Perhaps he was determined to pursue his investigations in the way he saw fit and unfettered by oversight. This would not have been out of character. At least twice he took others to task for treading on his turf, from the high and mighty—the national government in the person of none other than long-time Prime Minister Sir John A Macdonald—to the lowly—fellow members of the department.

Eighteen months after the bogus assassination

plot, the Prime Minister, strangely still a true believer, informed the House of Commons, on the same day he denied any intention of inviting Jamaica into Confederation, that the arrest of the Halifax dynamiters was due to information obtained by the Dominion government. The next day, Power's declaration that the Prime Minister's statement was a "barefaced falsehood" was national news. *The Globe* (Toronto) quoted him extensively: "We never received any information whatever from the Dominion Government, or any other government, or any other man and the arrest was wholly worked up by ourselves." This is patently false. The federal government had warned Halifax officials of possible Fenian designs in the spring of 1882. Absurdly, Power is claiming to be the sole discoverer of a plot that never existed. However, more important is Power's pugnacity when it came to sharing the glory or surrendering his turf. Detective Power would pull rank on anyone, even the Prime Minister, if his prerogatives, privileges or talents were threatened. He concluded that any claim of federal credit was "a misstatement that ought to be strongly contradicted," even if it came from the venerated and already beknighted Sir John A Macdonald.

Further proof of Power's sense of self-worth and privilege is evident in his other appearance in the Police Committee minutes. Evidence of his growing influence is provided by the fact that he was neither present at, nor even named during the meeting in question, although his hands are all over one specific motion. At the Police Committee meeting held on Friday, February 5, 1886 a motion was passed stating, "no member of the Force were [*sic*] allowed to engage in detective work without Permission of the Marshall." Its implicit corollary is that only Detective Power is to engage in detective work. Unlike most officers who appeared as the accused before the Police Committee and expected judgement, Power managed to manoeuvre the Police Committee into reasserting his domain and, implicitly, his independence of action. Not surprisingly, the bad detective was at least as concerned about preserving his jurisdiction, feeding his self-esteem and fostering his media image, as he was about intangibles like truth and justice.

With his hard, driving ambition and inflated sense of self, Power threw himself into the competition to replace Marshall Cotter when the department was reorganised. Whether it was memories of the 1889 expense problems or, as McGahan suggests, resentment amongst his fellow officers and the politicians, for his grandstanding, inflated public image and pomposity, the fact of the matter is Power was denied the highest job in the department in a bitter battle. These days elections seem fraught with malfeasance. Gerrymandering, ballot box stuffing (or its electronic counterpart), foreign interference and 'hanging chads' have all been contentious issues in modern elections across the globe. In 1892 the manoeuvring around the election of Halifax's new police chief equalled any of these contemporary examples of election tampering.

As noted earlier, the reorganisation of the Halifax Police Department also entailed personnel changes. Most importantly, Marshall Cotter was put out to pasture while retaining his title, and his deputy was superannuated. This left an open competition for their successors. Applications were accepted, however skullduggery emerged before they were even considered. The requirement that applicants be under the age of 30 had disappeared from the job qualifications and no one would take responsibility for the omission.

Proceeding nonetheless, the Police Committee had four names to consider when it convened in April, 1893. Experienced outsider Robert Rawlings, local radical gadfly John Naylor and two officers from the department, John O'Sullivan and Detective Power. Rawlings had 21 years' service in the British Army and time on the Moncton Police Department, where he had also served as the Canada Temperance Act (1878) prosecutor, as experience. Naylor was a strange bird with seemingly boundless energy and diverse interests. His wealth was based on real estate. According to the *Dictionary of Canadian Biography*, "In 1895 he had, in addition to 136 houses and 220 building lots for sale in the city, listings for 180 farms around the province and numerous houses in the country towns."

This property, and employment as a real estate agent and broker, did not prevent him from working variously as a liquor inspector, census enumerator, street cleaner and poultry farmer, all while serving as the secretary of the Nova Scotia Society for the Prevention of Cruelty (SPC), from its inception late in 1876 until his resignation in 1899. Not to be confused with the SPCA, it offered relief to indigent women, victims of domestic abuse and orphans. Power had two year's seniority over O'Sullivan, but O'Sullivan had the advantage, as a sergeant rather than a detective, of having remained in the chain of command and gained more supervisory experience. Ultimately, the Police Committee chairman Mayor George E Boak forwarded the committee's recommendation for chief, Detective Nicholas Power, to the council as a whole.

In the two weeks before the council considered a successor more horses entered the race: Henry D Rankine, G S M Gibson, Detective Peter Carroll, of Pictou, Kings County and former Ward 3 Alderman William F Pickering. Despite being nominated by Ward 4 Alderman John F Ryan, Pickering insisted to *The Herald* he had no interest in the job. Then the issue of eligibility and requirements came up for discussion. Some councillors concurred with the council recorder who opined that a man over 30 could be chosen, but only if he was already a member of the force. This interpretation, passed by a vote of nine to seven, narrowed the field to five: Carroll, Gibson, Naylor, O'Sullivan and Power. Ever-combative Alderman Hubley threw a wrench in the works. He demanded documentary proof that Carroll and Gibson were under 30. When they were unable to produce it, as few could in the 19th century, they were ruled ineligible. The council was left with the maverick Detective Power, the radical outsider Naylor and the stalwart Sergeant John O'Sullivan.

It took three ballots for a winner to emerge, but it was clear early that it wouldn't be Power. On the first ballot four aldermen supported him, half of O'Sullivan's eight votes and one less than Naylor. On the second ballot Power got only two votes, Aldermen Allen and Wallace having shifted their support to Naylor. On the final ballot Allen moved again, giving O'Sullivan a majority of nine of the 17 votes. Sergeant John O'Sullivan was chief of the newly reorganised Halifax Police Department. Of the five councillors on the Police Committee Duggan and Wallace supported Power; McFatridge and Hubley backed O'Sullivan; and, Outhit championed Naylor. The committee was clearly divided and for it to have recommended Power he must have had the support of its sixth member, Mayor Boak. However, as mayor, he did not participate in the council vote and clearly his preference meant nothing. On the final ballot the bad detective only received two of 15 votes, finishing a distant third in a three-horse race.

It is impossible to distinguish why his selection was so widely opposed, but clearly it was. A variety of reasons can easily be postulated, however. The aldermen might very well have concluded that Power's public image would have given him leverage and too much influence in the role of chief. Memories of his obstinate refusal to name sources three years earlier would have heightened this anxiety. Rumours of resentment of his inflated profile among his fellow officers might have reached the aldermen. They may have disliked him personally. Regardless of motive, the council clearly wanted anyone other than Power to become chief.

It is rather easier to suggest the bad detective's response to his thrashing. He was unaccustomed to losing and he had been beaten badly and publicly. He had been found wanting and the 'Man who saved the Prince' was not comfortable having his abilities, credentials and qualifications questioned. Undoubtedly, his countenance revealed nothing and his ramrod-straight back remained. Inside one can see his self-righteous rectitude mutating. He was the 'Man who saved the Prince', obviously the most qualified candidate. His inflated sense of self would have made the wound deeper and fester longer. His penchant for media attention matched with his resentment would have spawned an 'I'll show them attitude'. If it was ordained that, going forward, he remain a detective, the 'Man who saved the Prince' was determined to make his mark in that role and keep his name in the headlines and his exploits on the front pages.

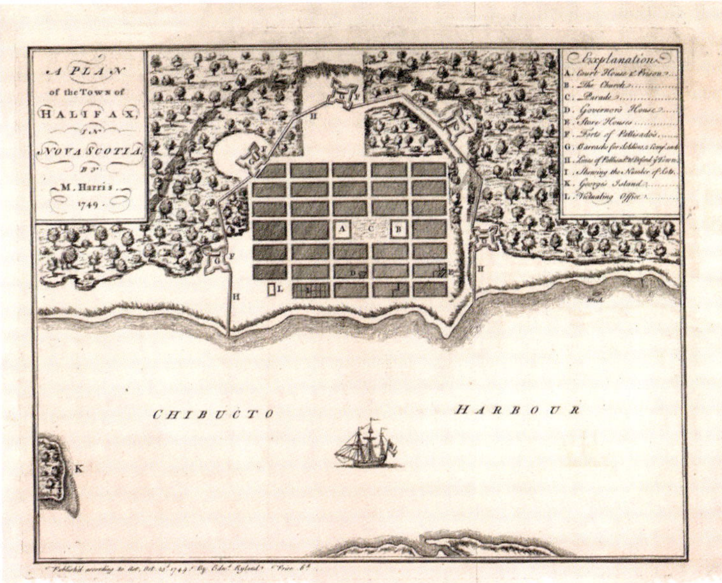

'A Plan of the Town of Halifax in Nova Scotia by M Harris, 1749.' The fort at the upper centre of the map is located atop Citadel Hill. Feature 'H' is the line of palisades running from there to the shoreline of The Narrows (identified on this map as Chibucto Harbour). LIBRARY OF CONGRESS, GEOGRAPHY AND MAP DIVISION.

This sketch of the young Prince George as a midshipman or 'middie' appeared in *The Globe* (Toronto) on Monday, August 8, 1883 as the Prince and his party toured Ontario. Less than three months later Detective Power would vault to fame as the 'Man who saved the Prince'.

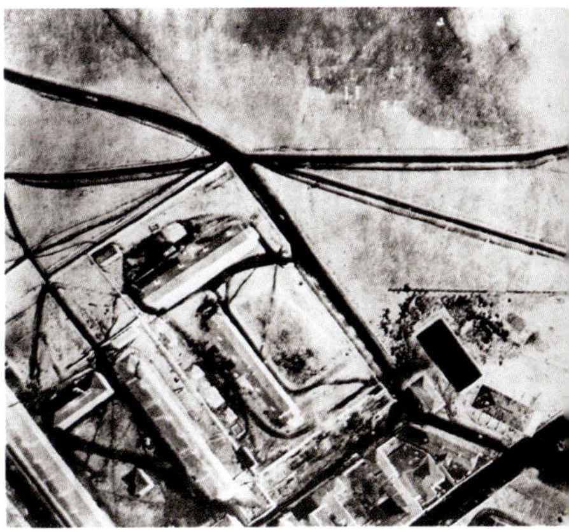

This remarkable aerial photograph of the Halifax Citadel was taken by a British Army balloonist in 1883, the very year Power's fictional, foundation myth established him as the 'Man who saved the Prince'. CANADA DEPT. OF NATIONAL DEFENCE/ LIBRARY AND ARCHIVES CANADA/C-3521

When Fenian Patrick J Whelan assassinated Thomas D'Arcy McGee in Ottawa on April 7, 1868, his funeral procession was massive and mourners filled the streets. After multiple assaults by armed Fenians, Canadians deeply distrusted, passionately hated and feared the Fenians. When Detective Power claimed to have uncovered a Fenian plot and became the 'Man who saved the Prince', he was preaching to the choir. GEORGE MARTIN/LIBRARY AND ARCHIVES CANADA/PA-165260

Looking north from Citadel Hill in 1887. The Bedford Basin is visible in the distance. Its superb natural harbour, protected by The Narrows, determined Halifax's location when it was established in 1749. CANADA PATENT AND COPYRIGHT OFFICE/LIBRARY AND ARCHIVES CANADA/PA-031176

In 1901 Prince George (the royal Power claimed to have saved) undertook the first royal tour of the Empire following the death of Queen Victoria. The Canadian leg ended in Halifax in October 1901. Chief O'Sullivan is pictured second from the left (it may be Deputy Chief Nickerson on the right) and RMS *Ophir,* royal yacht for the one tour and temporarily designated HMS *Ophir,* is in the background. The photograph was taken by renowned Canadian photographer William James Topley. WILLIAM JAMES TOPLEY/LIBRARY AND ARCHIVES CANADA/PA-012059

Barrington Street in Halifax, looking south from the corner of Sackville Street.
HENRY JOSEPH WOODSIDE/LIBRARY AND ARCHIVES CANADA/PA-016372

The Halifax Police Department assembled in front of their new station, in the basement of the recently built city hall in 1893 or 1894. Detective Power's imposing bulk is on the far right out of uniform, and the new chief, John O'Sullivan, taller but much thinner than Power, is on the far left. In the centre of the front row, with a double-breasted coat and prominent, dark moustache is Deputy Chief Charles Nickerson. IMAGE PROVIDED BY HALIFAX REGIONAL POLICE DEPARTMENT ARCHIVIST MARLENE MILLER.

INTELLIGENCE.

HALIFAX—ARRIVED.

WEDNESDAY, Oct 17.

...ner, Newfield, Guildford, from
...e Dagmar, Bertelson, Liverpool,
... Albion, Rode, Liverpool, G
...Culloch, Savanna-la Mar, Ja, to
Was in collision with Dutch
See local column
...unroe, St Thomas via Turks
& Co
...es, King, Bay St George, N F, to
...a & Co
...d, Labrador via Georgetown, P
...han. Reports left schr Verbena,
...rringtons Harbor on the 12th.
... Arnold, Lobrador, to Davis &
...h, Webber, Labrador, to Da is
...nier, Magdalen Islands.
...rson, Charlottetown, P E I.
..., Taylor, Pownal, P E I.
..., Cardigan Bridge, P E I.
...Bell, Grand River, P E I.
...ht, McDonald, Malpeque, P E I.
...on, Glawson, Ingonish.
..., Devoe, Little Bras d Or.
... Hayes, North Sydney.
... Giffin, Cow Bay.
...turn, Boudrot, Cow Bay.
..., Scattarie.
... L'Ardoise.
...e, River Bourgeoise,
...ke, River Bourgeoise.
...urke, River Bourgeoise.
...er, Pictou.
..., Pictou
..., Tor Bay

ARCHIBALD & CO., Sydney, C. B.
C. DWYER & CO., Pictou, N. S.
McDONALD, McDONALD & CO., Souris, P.E.I.
BOWRING BROTHERS, St. John's, N.F.

C. J. WYLDE,
General Agent for Nova Scotia.

my31 –6m tts ins

Important to Miners

The Subscribers have received a further supply of

Nobel's No. 1

RED DYNAMITE!

and are now prepared to supply the trade on the most favorable terms. This GENUINE and RELIABLE article is the

Most Powerful and Economical Explosive
FOR ALL KINDS OF
Mining and Quarrying Operations,

and miners will find it vastly superior to any other in the market.

Treble Charge Detonators, Fuse, Warming Pans.

and other requisites at lowest rates.
For descriptive pamphlets and other information apply to

F. D. CORBETT & CO.,
—SOLE AGENTS—
Nobel's Explosive Company
aug4

Oranges, Oranges.

WE offer for sale, to arrive by S. S. "BETA,"

Just received another lot of

SUPERIOR FUR GOOD...

This lot we have purchased under regular prices a... are offering at lowest rates.

SPLENDID VALUE...
Black Australian Opossum Cap...
Black Lynx Fur Capes. Lined Quilted Satin.

MUFFS, MUFFS, MUFF...

Lynx, Opossum, Genet, South Sea Seal.

The Duchess Pocket Muff.
The Czarina Pocket Muff.

Ladies' Misses and Childre... Gossmamer Waterproofs &c. &c.

oct 9 her

Price Reduced.

To arrive in a few days one car load "Lyma...
4 Barb Galvanised Steel

WIRE FENCING

While Power was whipping up hysteria about innocent miners being bomb-wielding, regicidal terrorists F D Corbett & Co, sole agents of Nobel's Explosive Company in Halifax, were targeting their dynamite advertising in *The Herald* at miners.

A Southside blue blood and one of the leading jurists of his generation, John David Sparrow Thompson, frequently crossed paths with Nic Power. As a Nova Scotia Supreme Court Justice in March 1884, two years before this photograph was taken, he declined to convict Power's alleged Fenian bombers to anything beyond six months for dynamite smuggling. TOPLEY STUDIO FONDS/LIBRARY AND ARCHIVES CANADA/PA-027084

A sketch of Jack Sheppard awaiting his execution in 1724, attributed to Sir James Thornhill. Ainsworth's novelisation of his life, published in 1839, and Lord William Russell's killer's claim that reading the book led him to murder, made Sheppard posthumously famous. He was a central meme in the late-Victorian obsession with murder and mayhem.

On New Year's Day, 1906, after 41 years' service, Detective Nicholas Power was promoted to chief of the department. His brief tenure would last less than two years.

During the 1870s, Sergeant Power, his wife Mary Jane and their growing family lived above this retail outlet at Clyde and Birmingham, in the heart of Schmidt's Ville. At the time it was a liquor store, but today it is 'the convenience that has everything at reasonable prices'. PHOTO BY AUTHOR.

The investigation into the murder of 14-year-old Annie Kempton in January 1896 concluded with the conviction and execution of Peter Wheeler, despite the fact that it was categorically impossible for him to have committed the crime. Newspaper illustrators, in an era before photojournalism, freely expressed their biases in their portrayals of Wheeler.

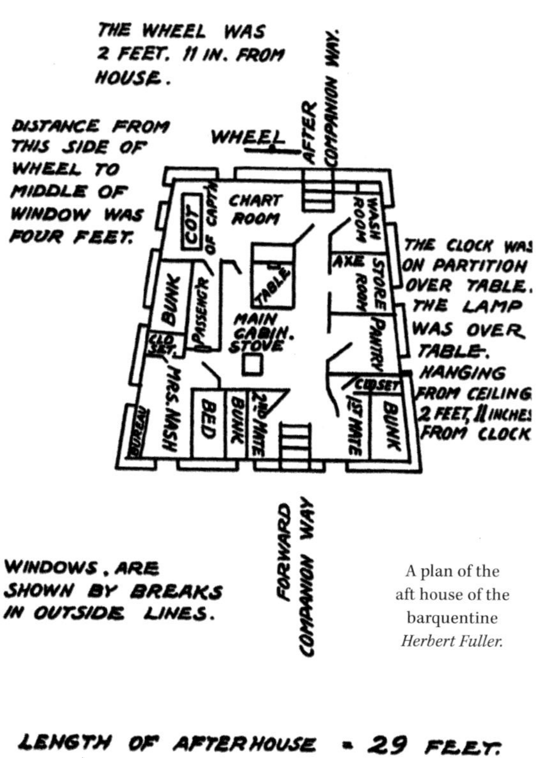

ROUGH SKETCH OF THE AFTER HOUSE INSIDE.

A plan of the aft house of the barquentine *Herbert Fuller.*

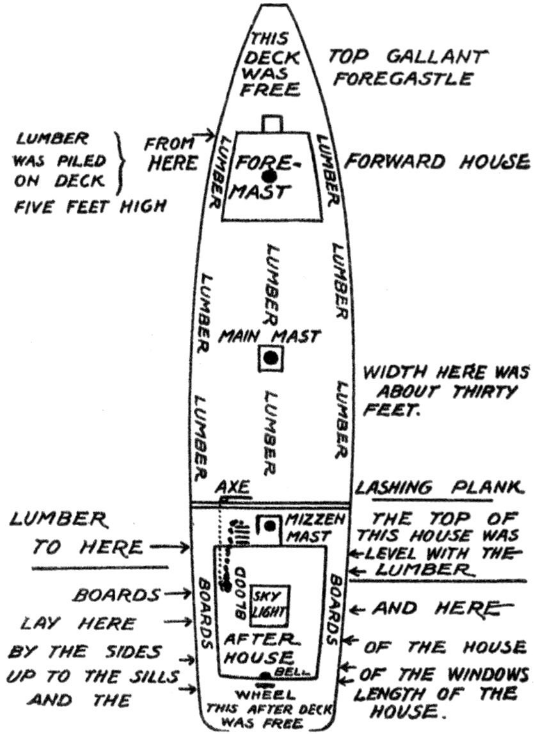

ROUGH SKETCH OF THE DECK.

A plan of the deck of the barquentine *Herbert Fuller*. One of the vessel's mates, Thomas Bram, was found guilty of the murders of its captain, Charles Nash, his wife Laura and the second mate, August Blomburg, in July 1896.

CHAPTER SIX

Peter Wheeler (1896)

THE EARLIEST execution in Halifax dates to 1749, the year the city was founded. The *Beaufort* was a privateer that arrived with the convoy of Governor Cornwallis carrying troops and tradesmen, including a butcher, a blacksmith and a carpenter. The Governor chose to hold his Governing Council meetings on board, so it remained until the end of the sailing season, only departing on October 27. Aboard the *Beaufort* in Bedford Basin, sailor Peter Carteel ran amok, killing the bosun's mate and wounding two other members of the crew.

After a Captain's Court he swung from the yardarm. In 1790, one of the first women executed in Halifax was drawn to the scaffold on a cart. The noose was placed around her neck and the drayman lashed the horse, leaving her behind, suspended. In pre-Confederation Canada executions were *ad hoc* local affairs. Legally, they were the responsibility of the local sheriff, although he could hire a proxy. Wildly popular, often temporarily doubling the population of the localities they were held in, they remained vernacular, unscientific, improvised and often gruesomely unsuccessful.

The margin of error was slim in hanging. A rope too light could break; a drop too long or a body too heavy could decapitate the condemned; and, if the jolt at the end of the drop was not abrupt enough to dislocate the vertebrae, the victim convulsed for agonising minutes as they slowly strangled. In at least one shocking instance the straps pinioning the doomed man's arms failed and the crowd watched him try to pull himself up the rope until his strength failed and he eventually suffocated.

It would be a quarter of a century after Confederation before the new Dominion government acted to rationalise and nationalise executions, replacing local amateurs with utilitarian consistency. John Radclive, Canada's first professional executioner, was placed on the federal payroll as a hangman by a Dominion order-in-council dated January 11, 1892, on the recommendation of the justice minister, Haligonian, the Honourable John Sparrow David Thompson, who introduced Canada's first federal criminal code later the same year.

Radclive claimed to have learned his trade under

British hangman William Marwood, having first practiced the craft in the Royal Navy hanging South Seas pirates, although there is no independent corroboration of these claims. Radclive started hanging convicts on the side in 1890 while living at various addresses in the Parkdale neighbourhood of Toronto and working as steward of the Sunnyside Rowing Club. When members learned of his moonlighting, they objected to having their libations served by a common hangman. Unemployed Radclive became Canada's first official executioner. A retainer of $750 annually and $50 per execution plus expenses secured his services. Unlike England, Radclive was not permitted to sell the rope by the inch, although he was entitled to the dead prisoner's haberdashery, as was customary.

The journalist Hector Willoughby Charlesworth recalls discussing Radclive's vocation with "the very genial Englishman" in his memoir *Candid Chronicles*. "'If they're heavy I drops 'em; if they're light I jerks 'em up.' I was very slender at the time, and he added: 'Now if I was 'angin' you I would jerk you up,' and he indicated the spot on my neck where he would place the knot." Perhaps surprisingly, Radclive was a firm believer in the 'jerk 'em up' or reverse hanging method early in his career. Rather than dropping the victim down to tighten the noose and cause death, the condemned was jerked up when a counterweight was let free to fall. This bizarre approach avoided construction of a scaffold, which was expensive, time-consuming, rarely required again and difficult to repurpose. A counterweight, pulleys attached overhead and an axe were all that was required for a reverse hanging.

The sheriff of Digby, Nova Scotia on the Bay of Fundy coast, Benjamin Van Blarcom, apparently both parsimonious and something of a home handyman, declined to pay the federal government's $50 fee and Radclive's expenses or spend money having a scaffold constructed to dispatch convicted murderer Peter Wheeler in the fall of 1896. On July 7, he assured the *Morning Chronicle*'s correspondent that he could "hang Wheeler with good grace". Deciding to construct the apparatus to execute Wheeler himself, and in his own abode, he adopted Radclive's 'I jerks 'em up' method, although Radclive had abandoned it a few years earlier.

Van Blarcom's residence was within the jail grounds, which was convenient as the federal government had recently ended the spectacle of public executions. Initially moved from the public realm to the prison grounds in 1868, they were still carried out on an elevated scaffold visible beyond the walls. However, by the 1890s discretion had trumped the spectacle and a pit was often dug under the gallows precluding the need to construct an elevated platform.

Van Blarcom found an almost ready-made solution at hand, his front porch. Conveniently, it had a small room, possibly a root cellar, hidden from public view, beneath it. A hole was cut in the floor of the porch and a pulley attached to the porch ceiling. The rope, with a noose on its end, was strung from the cellar through the hole in its ceiling (the porch floor) and over the pulley, affixed to the porch ceiling beams. A 500lb counterweight, attached to the ceiling of the porch by a second lead, was tied to the noose rope also. The noose was placed around Wheeler's neck as he stood in the cellar. At the appointed minute the rope securing the counterweight to the porch ceiling was cut, jerking Wheeler up towards the cellar ceiling, killing him.

Or so went the theory. In Wheeler's case, Van Blarcom's jerry-built, Rube Goldberg contraption worked, eventually. To be precise, it took 28 minutes for Peter Wheeler to strangle to death according to John Daley's excruciating "Coroners Report on the death of Peter Wheeler" prepared immediately following the surreptitious execution in the early hours of September 9, 1896. For the worse, Wheeler was an innocent man. Despite unfortunate circumstances, it was categorically impossible for him to have committed the murder for which he was 'hanged by the neck till dead', or, in this instance, 'jerked up to the ceiling till strangled'.

The case against him did not follow from the facts. The evidence was twisted and wrenched into conformity with the presumption that Wheeler was guilty of murder. The leading proponent of this theory was Detective Power, called in due to the heinous and serious nature of the crime. The bull moose of a man's reputation preceded him. The pronouncements of the 'Man who saved the Prince' would be treated like stone tablets of truth and his megaphone was the press. Early and often, months before Wheeler was before a court, Power would assure journalists that Wheeler was the fiend responsible and that he held incontrovertible evidence of Wheeler's guilt. Months before he faced a jury of his peers, he had been convicted by Detective Power, journalists and the public.

The story starts on Monday, January 27, 1896 outside the hamlet of Bear River, Nova Scotia. The town is located southeast of Digby on the Bear River, approximately four miles inland from its mouth on the south coast of the Bay of Fundy. *A Geography and History of the County of Digby, Nova Scotia* by Isaiah W Wilson (1900) describes Bear River as "the principal Village in Hillsburgh, carrying on an extensive trade in lumber, cherries, West India produce, and other commodities."

On the Monday night in question, 14-year-old Annie Kempton was home alone. Her mother was away at work in the Massachusetts textile mills, her brother and father were spending weeknights at the lumber camp where they were employed. On Tuesday morning Peter Wheeler was dispatched by the mistress of his boarding house, Tillie Comeau, to the neighbouring Kempton farm to fetch the day's supply of fresh milk. Not a local and of indeterminate origins, Wheeler had resided at the Comeau boarding house for a dozen years alternating between going to sea, casual labour and trapping and hunting. That morning he had the misfortune of discovering the badly beaten, possibly sexually assaulted, body of Annie on the floor. Clad in only a nightshirt she was surrounded by evidence of a struggle. Case knives and a blood-stained billet of firewood lay beside her and the walls were blood-stained. There was a bloody handprint on a windowsill and blood-stained footprints trailed off into the distance behind the house. Covering her with a coat and briefly searching the house, Wheeler immediately raised the alarm.

Born in 1869, Wheeler, admittedly a queer bird, was Mauritian, although he often claimed to be otherwise. Locals had, and the press would, speculate on him being Portuguese, Spanish, Australian *ad infinitum*. He was not only literate, but multilingual despite having had no formal schooling. He had gone to sea at the age of eight, aboard the barquentine *Lochiel*, captained by his uncle, David Stevenson Wheeler, and risen to first mate, a not inconsiderable achievement requiring not only literacy but knowledge of mathematics, astronomy and other sciences above and beyond seamanship. His travels at sea took him through Europe and to the West Indies. Coming ashore in Digby in October 1884 he ventured to Bear River at the invitation of a shipmate who had family there.

A dozen years later he was still in Bear River and according to locals "he was a quiet, inoffensive fellow" the *Herald* reported. Nonetheless, his ancestry, intelligence and multilingualism, coupled with his relatively 'recent' arrival in the community and lack of extended family in the neighbourhood clearly marked him as an outsider. Rumours of an inappropriate relationship with his landlady, unmarried but a mother and morally ambiguous herself, further muddied the waters. Perhaps it would be most accurate to describe him as admitted to the community, but neither entirely accepted nor fully a member.

The newspapers immediately realised the appeal of the story and leapt head first, facts be damned. The next day *The Herald* had Annie's age as 15 not 14, and if such a thing is possible *The Digby Weekly Courier* managed to get it even more wrong, informing readers, in one and the same article, that Annie was both 15 and 16. These errors did nothing to preclude chilling headlines and leads. *The Herald* called it "Bear River's Diabolical TRAGEDY" and, in the lead, described Annie's body as "Brutally Mangled".

Interest in the crime was not restricted to Nova Scotia. Across the Bay of Fundy the case attracted intense interest. From New Brunswick, *The St John Daily Sun* dispatched its ace crime reporter, 51-year-old Robert Payne, to the scene. Initially, the case merited only minor notice nationally with *The Toronto Evening Star* erroneously reporting that the victim had been 'outraged' on January 29. However, by the first of February it was garnering headlines nationally.

At the centre of these stories was the omnipresent and

seemingly omniscient Detective Power. Upon discovery of the body, local authorities immediately sent out a call for assistance to the provincial Attorney General. They requested the services of the vaunted Detective Nicholas Power, presently dealing with another capital offence in New Glasgow. Before Power had even arrived in the community on Wednesday, January 29, *The Herald* was reporting that he was sure to turn up the culprit by "looking at different channels". On the first day of February, *The Globe*'s lead featured Detective Power's revelations. The murder of Annie Kempton and the press put Power at the centre of the case before he had even arrived and he immediately inserted himself even deeper.

Before Power arrived, the local authorities convened a coroner's inquest to determine the cause and manner of death. A list of witnesses was compiled and a jury empanelled. The inquest convened at 2pm on January 28, only hours after Annie's lifeless body was discovered. It was held in Bear River's new Oakdene Academy, a combination schoolhouse, city hall and public meeting place that had cost the princely sum of $8,000. Standing room only was the order of the day. This speed may seem unusual in light of the delays and long grind of modern judicial procedures. However, it was par for the course in the late Victorian era.

The local coroner was Bear River doctor Lewis Johnstone Lovett. A Maritimer, originally from Kentville and a graduate of Acadia University, he received his medical degree from the New York University School of Medicine. He had followed his heart to Bear River, marrying Josephine Troop Marshall, daughter of a prominent, local merchant. He planned to establish his practice on the ground floor of a brand-new Empire-style home looking down on the town, financed by his father-in-law, Alpheus Marshall Esq. Connected by marriage to the local elite, young and energetic, he was rapidly earning the respect of the community. He would go on to serve as President of the Bear River Board of Trade and a quarter of a century after these events he would be elected as Member of Parliament for Digby and Annapolis in Prime Minister Mackenzie King's first Liberal federal government from 1921 to 1925.

However, in 1896 he was not yet 30, relatively new to the community and this was his first coroner's inquest. As competent a physician as he was, he was a neophyte in the world of murder and had no specialist training in pathology or forensics. He had no experience to draw on and a limited understanding of the role and responsibilities of a coroner. Unfortunately, while it does not seem to have impacted on his conduct of the inquest, youthful deference and inexperience tainted his conclusions. They set poor Peter Wheeler, an innocent man, on the road to his death in a root cellar under Benjamin Van Blarcom's front porch.

A coroner's inquest has no role in the criminal justice process beyond one simple contribution, determining the *cause* of death. It can conclude that an individual was asphyxiated or died of an embolism or loss of blood as a result of a stab wound. But, in cases of homicide it can only determine the cause, not the culprit. Further, this determination is to be based on physical evidence and forensic science.

At the inquiry Lovett's first witness was Peter Wheeler, since he had discovered the body. As the first to testify, with no press yet to report, Detective Power not yet in town and Annie's body barely cold, Wheeler seems to have had no inkling that he was about to become a suspect. He testified he had crossed paths with Annie during the day and she had asked him to tell his landlady, Tillie Comeau, she did not need company that night as a friend was staying with her. He did so and provided an account of his movements for the rest of the evening. The friend, Gracie Morraine, subsequently testified that she had made no such arrangement with Annie.

Immediately, the question of who was lying arose. Had Wheeler lied to get Annie alone? Had Annie lied simply to have the freedom of an adolescent night alone? Or, was Gracie Morraine lying for reasons unknown? It seems that the mood at the inquest, and popular opinion, suddenly shifted against the outsider, Peter Wheeler, the man in, but not of, the community. He had deceitfully arranged that she would be alone that evening so he could advance his lustful designs. Physical proximity coupled with social and ethnic distance made Peter Wheeler a ready scapegoat.

The key testimony on the second afternoon of the inquiry was presented by Bear River's second physician, long-time resident, Dr Robert J Ellison. Annie had been a patient since her birth and to him, Bear River's only physician who was not the coroner, fell the task of performing the autopsy. The day before the inquest and autopsy had proceeded concurrently, now, Ellison had the unpleasant task of enumerating his findings to the jury. He identified two clusters of wounds. Two blunt force wounds to the head, presumably inflicted with the bloody billet, had rendered her unconscious. However, the cause of death was the three deep gashes on her neck. In addition, the body was covered with numerous lacerations and contusions deemed to be a result of the struggle the overturned furniture and disarray of the room attested to. In the constrained public manner of the late-Victorian age, the good doctor assured one and all, even as they gasped, that she had not been 'outraged' as the "vagina was all right".

Dr Ellison also offered an estimate as to the time of death. He had begun his examination one hour after Lovett gavelled the inquiry to order the day before. He estimated that the body had been deceased 13 hours at that time, making the time of death 2am on Tuesday, January 28. Allowing for a margin of error he testified that death had occurred between midnight and 4am. Following Ellison's testimony, a plethora of locals testified to having seen Peter Wheeler in the vicinity of the

Kempton house in the late afternoon on Monday. Representing the Crown was Assistant Crown Attorney J M Owen. Throughout the inquest he pressed the theory that Annie had been murdered in the late afternoon, coincident with the time that witnesses testified Peter had been seen near the Kemptons'.

In the spirit of the times journalists felt free to speculate before the doctor's testimony and, in many instances, sustain errors subsequently. Newspapers across Canada reported that Annie had been 'outraged'. While the story was eventually dropped, retractions were unheard of in the age. Unfortunately, that was not all *The Herald* got wrong. On January 29, the day after the murder, before the inquest had finished and cause of death had even been determined, its lead read: "Her Lifeless Body, Brutally Mangled Found in Her Lonely Home. Peter Wheeler, Who Made the Discovery, Arrested on Suspicion of Having Committed the Awful Crime." In fact, the inquiry had not concluded, and Wheeler had not yet been arrested. Late on Wednesday the jury retired to consider its verdict.

After deliberating for only a short period, the coroner and jury returned. Lovett read the verdict: "We do upon oath say that Annie Kempton, between the hour of 5 in the afternoon of Monday, the 27th day of January, and the hour of 8 o'clock in the morning of Tuesday, 28th day of January, aforesaid was violently assaulted and struck on the forehead and head several heavy blows and had her throat cut in several places, causing her death. And we further say that said Annie Kempton was thereby feloniously killed and murdered at her father's residence in Bear River." Annie's death was murder, a result of her throat being cut after being battered by a billet of firewood.

For the most part, the inexperienced coroner had acquitted himself admirably. However, he had fudged the time of death. He had left so wide a window that any theory could fit the bill, including the unlikely theory that Annie had been murdered on the Monday at approximately 5pm and not late, after 10.30pm and perhaps even after midnight, in the early hours of the Tuesday. There is no apparent explanation for this as it directly contradicts Dr Ellison's testimony as to time of death. This is peculiar, a doctor dismissing medical evidence: particularly as it came from an esteemed, elder colleague. It is impossible not to wonder if Power spoke to him and pressed his position. This theory is encouraged when one considers the coda to the verdict.

A decidedly deadly error overshadowed this sleight of hands of the clock. Unfortunately, for reasons that will forever remain known only to Lovett himself, he could not get while the getting was good. And the proper conclusion to the inquest included an improper codicil that sent Peter Wheeler off on his fatal journey, "And we suspect Peter Wheeler of Bear River in the county of Digby, yeoman, to be guilty of the said murder of

Annie Kempton."This statement, the naming of a suspect, was way outside of the coroner's wheelhouse. Today, in Canada it could never occur. A coroner could not insert himself into the naming of a suspect, let alone the process of determining guilt or innocence. Wheeler, not yet represented by a lawyer, had no one to object to this inexplicable and unproven announcement. Illegitimately Wheeler had been officially identified as the primary suspect within 48 hours of the crime.

Detective Power arrived in Bear River on Wednesday morning, hours before the coroner's inquest delivered its loaded verdict. He promptly consulted with Crown Attorney Owen during the inquest's lunch break. Mere hours later, having neither attended the inquest nor visited the crime scene, Power assured the reporter for the *Courier Weekly* "that he had no doubt himself that Wheeler was guilty". Apparently, the reporter concurred, writing: "If he is guilty, as certainly is very probable, he is a remarkably cool and audacious villain." A more backhanded compliment is hard to imagine. Power was so confident of his assertion that he arrested Wheeler hours before the coroner's inquiry had delivered even a cause of death. The unlikely assertion in the coroner's report that Wheeler was the primary suspect was merely an affirmation of Power's theory. Similarly, the line of questioning that Owen pursued at the inquiry was concurrent to Power's assertions. On every level a consensus was forming that Peter Wheeler was guilty.

On Friday, the last day of January, Detective Power announced his conclusions to the press. On that day Power had escorted Wheeler as he was moved from Bear River to the jail in Digby. Alone with the prisoner during the trip Power hinted to the press that Wheeler had revealed certain facts that proved his guilt. Further, Power suggested that they affirmed his theory that Wheeler "struck Annie with the club when he was at the house about 6 o'clock," according to *The Globe*. The *Courier*, *Herald* and *Daily Sun* all concurred, Peter Wheeler was the culprit. Allowing some hometown pride to slip in, *The Chronicle* confidently announced: "Detective Power is on top." If the erudite Detective Power, the detective who saved the Prince's life, knew Wheeler was guilty, that was good enough for the newshounds. They freely and frequently fed Power's theories to the public. The issue was decided before Peter Wheeler was charged, let alone tried.

The Globe article is very interesting. Based on conversations with Power it states: "It is now very strongly suspected that Wheeler is the murderer of Annie Kempton." It then goes on to detail conversations Power held with the prisoner during their trip to Digby that day, including the hint that certain revelations, not yet suitable for release to the public, had been made by Wheeler. "The theory of those who believe Wheeler is guilty is that he struck Annie with the club when he was at the house about 6 o'clock," it concludes. This reads more like a press release than journalism. It is little more than a distillation of Power's opinions about the case. It captures the tangled relationship between Power and the media. The spectacular nature of the crimes he was involved in, coupled with his personal reputation, sold newspapers. Simply summarising his pronouncements made for easy copy and kept one on the great man's good side. This is not some hokey, small-town weekly. Published in Toronto, Ontario *The Globe* was one of the most influential daily newspapers in Canada at the time and it happily and uncritically published Detective Power's judgements.

Newspapers closer to home were even more adoring. A feature interview in the *Chronicle* published on Monday, February 3, was entitled simply The Detective's Story. It put Power front and centre in the coverage of the case and allowed him to outline, with bombastic certitude, the course of events and evidence that clearly established Peter Wheeler's guilt beyond a shadow of a doubt.

The first week of this case was a carnival. From the moment the body was discovered the crime scene was visited by neighbours, gawkers and amateur detectives. The coroner's inquest produced an outrageous conclusion, going beyond cause of death to name a suspect. The newshounds made up wild accusations and pointed fingers while frequently getting the facts wrong. Like wildfire reporting on the sensational story raced across the country. Titillating hints of sexual improprieties and miscegenation only increased the appeal of the story to reporters and readers alike. The arrival of the internationally renowned Detective Power ratcheted up the spotlight.

Locals were not unaware of this. Out of the blue, the Honourable Wallace A Purdy, a local magistrate, and apparently a media maven to challenge Power, saw an opening and announced that a police magistrate's examination was necessary. He was within his rights to do so, it was legal, but it was not required, other than to assuage Purdy's ego. Its redundancy is made plain by one simple fact, its witness list was identical to Lovett's prior inquest. However, it must have done a world of good for Purdy's sense of self, being held in the Bear River Exhibition Hall, the community's only assembly hall larger than the academy occupied by the coroner's inquest.

Gratifying as it must have been for Purdy, the police magistrate's examination added little new and even then, only more so. Purdy's folly only added to Wheeler's predicament when he opened it by asking how Wheeler pleaded, guilty or innocent. Wheeler was not in a court and he hadn't even been charged with a crime yet! This ridiculous preamble served only to reinforce the idea that Wheeler was guilty, and, as one scribe put it, "a fiendish beast".

Even worse for Wheeler, memories seemed to sharpen with the passage of time. As the consensus built around his guilt, acquaintances and neighbours were suddenly overflowing with unkind remembrances of Wheeler's lewd remarks and new, modified or enriched memories of the events leading up to Annie's demise and Wheeler's movements, actions and appearance during those hours. The redundant testimony also kept the crime, and Detective Power's apparent resolution of it, in the news still longer.

Purdy's caprice, befitting its setting more exhibition than examination, offered Bear Riverites opportunities to embellish their stories and sustain their place in the spotlight. It allowed Power to continue promoting his astounding ratiocination and conclusions. It sold newspapers. For Peter Wheeler it was the second step on his trip to the great beyond.

Twice he had stood before legal, but extra judicial proceedings. At the first, the coroner's inquest, he had testified willingly without benefit of counsel. Unrepresented, there was also no cross-examination of any of the witnesses. Finally, Coroner Lovett had gone way beyond his mandate when he not only determined the cause of death, but also named him as the primary suspect. At Purdy's police examination Wheeler had representation and was not compelled to testify. However, the stream of witnesses mirrored Lovett's view, many merely exaggerating their earlier evidence and none were subject to cross-examination. It served only to keep the story in the headlines and before the public, and the story was Detective Power's conclusion that Peter Wheeler was the murderer.

With Wheeler cooling his heels in the Digby jail, interest in the case quickly faded, if only briefly. Wheeler was to be tried at the Digby Summer Sessions of the Superior Court. Then, on May 7, Dwight Ruggles, representing Wheeler, requested a change of venue, arguing that it would be impossible to find an untainted jury in Bear River. A host of newspaper articles establishing the fact and notarised statements from local notables attesting to this opinion made the outcome inevitable. One of the notarised statements asserted that one of the coroner's inquest jurors had been heard to say "of course the Goddamned bastard killed her". Two weeks later Justice Townshend acceded to Ruggle's petition and Wheeler's trial was moved from Digby to Kentville, 80 miles east.

A change of venue of only 80 miles seems so futile as to be silly. The crime and subsequent coroner's inquiry and police examination had made the front page of every newspaper in the province. One could go so far as to say that it made news across the entire country. This minor change of venue serves only to demonstrate how far the criminal justice system had fallen behind the ongoing communication revolution brought on by railroads and the telegraph. Peter Wheeler's jury pool was well and truly tainted, whether his trial was to be held in Digby or Kentville. As meaningless as the gesture was, it allowed the entire legal caravan to get the show on the road. One can only but imagine that the great detective awaited, with anticipation, his star turn at the trial

First, Peter Wheeler had to actually, finally, be charged with a crime. On June 9, more than four months after his arrest, a grand jury was empanelled in Kentville and brought down formal charges. His trial began on June 26. The setting could not compare with the earlier extralegal proceedings. The Kentville courthouse had burned to the ground in 1849 and never been rebuilt. Two drafty warehouses by the railroad served; one as the courthouse, one as the jail.

Peter Wheeler made the short walk between the two each morning and late afternoon. Despite the summer trial, the improvised heating system in the makeshift courthouse would provide a moment of black humour, both literally and figuratively. An overhead chimney pipe collapsed. Full of a winter's worth of soot it left the prosecutors looking like they had on blackface. The accused was reported to have remarked that now the trial was a 'real' minstrel show.

The undignified setting aside, *gravitas* was amply provided by judge Charles James Townshend. Appointed to the Supreme Court (by Dominion Attorney General John David Sparrow Thompson) in 1887, his biographer states that "by blood, outlook, religion, and education, Charles Townshend was a true specimen of the old-regime elite in the Maritimes." Wheeler continued to be represented by Dwight Ruggles. Now available, the region's leading Crown, A J Copp, took over the prosecution from J M Owen.

Correctly expecting a mob scene, the makeshift courthouse's doors did not swing open until shortly before 10am. With a rush the public gallery was filled in minutes. The throng was so deep the bailiffs and witnesses had trouble getting into the courtroom. A large section of the gallery had been set aside for the newspapermen, but even with special consideration it was also overflowing. Peter Wheeler and Annie Kempton were back in the news and, if they were back in the news, so was Detective Power. The trial wasn't just news. True to the dictum 'if it bleeds, it leads' the trial, and by extension Detective Power, were front page news nationally.

Detective Power did not take the stand until the third day of the trial, the first two being taken up with opening statements and witnesses heard previously at the inquest and police examination. Importantly, multiple witnesses testified to seeing Wheeler in the neighbourhood of the Kempton house in the late afternoon. Detective Power had primed the public for his appearance with the complicity of the newspapers. They had repeatedly broadcast his assertions that he had incontrovertible evidence of Wheeler's guilt, evidence that could only, but would be, in due course, revealed at trial. On Saturday, drawing himself up to his full height, adopting the martial bearing that made his bulk more imposing still, he strode to the witness box as the court opened its afternoon session.

He testified to his arrival on the morning of Wednesday,

January 29 and immediately meeting with prosecutor Owen, concluding that Wheeler was the most likely suspect. Further, he told the *Yarmouth News* later "the atrocious crime must have been committed between the hours of 5 and 6 o'clock on Monday evening, as it was shown clearly that he was seen going in the direction of the [Kempton] house at that time."

Detective Power testified that tracks he had found in the snow, leading from the Kempton house past their barn and into the woods towards Wheeler's residence, the Comeau boarding house, matched Wheeler's footwear. Breathlessly, *The Digby Weekly Courier* reported he "produced a pair of larrigans [a vernacular knee-high boot of oiled leather with a moccasin foot, worn by lumbermen and trappers, popular in the region in the 19th century] taken off the prisoner and fitted them in the footmarks. They fitted the marks perfectly in length and breadth." It further assured readers, "The witness [Power] was on the scene at daylight and made a careful investigation." Power concluded his testimony about footprints noting "I found no marks in the immediate vicinity other than those I have spoken of."

He also testified that, suspiciously, Peter Wheeler had repeatedly excused any blood on his clothes as coming from rabbits he had snared and tied to his belt. To Power, who could find very little blood, this indicated fear that blood from the victim might be found. At the time forensics could not conclusively test for blood, let alone differentiate between human and animal blood. Nonetheless, it was evidence enough for the bad detective.

Power's recreation of the crime was quite detailed. Wheeler had a motive in frustrated sexual desire. He had the opportunity at the supper hour on Monday evening. The method, affirmed by the autopsy, was a blow with a billet of firewood to render the victim unconscious and the subsequent slashing of her neck. Further, there was evidence of his surreptitious flight behind the barn and through the woods to his boarding house. In the manner of the board game known as 'Clue' or 'Cluedo', it was Peter Wheeler, in the Kempton house, with the knife at 5pm.

A significant tangent in terms of forensic science also arose during Power's cross-examination, one that figures significantly in a future case of Power's. Bloody knives were found at the crime scene and there was a bloody handprint on a windowsill. Ruggles asked if Power had examined them for 'fingermarks' (fingerprints in modern terms). Comparison of fingerprints for identification purposes was in its infancy at the time, widely known and often employed, but not always accepted, as evidence. It would be the first decade of the 20th century before they were universally accepted by courts. Sherlock Holmes did not use fingerprint evidence, until he returned to life in the pages of *The Strand* in September 1903 after an apparently fatal fall at the hands of Dr Moriarity had seemed to end his life a few years earlier. Challenged about his investigative methods Power, perfectly in character, blustered. Of course, he had not examined any fingermarks, the science behind them was discredited. As a scientific detective he did not rely on spurious investigative methods. As we shall see, only weeks later, he would argue the exact opposite: that an attempt to destroy potential fingermark evidence was an implicit acknowledgement of guilt.

For the defence Ruggles chose to call no witnesses, believing cross-examination had been adequate to introduce 'reasonable doubt' of Wheeler's guilt or, accepting the inevitable, realising that Peter Wheeler's situation was hopeless; that he was already walking dead. His final address to the jury occupied less than an hour. He outlined the diverse evidence that contradicted Power's narrative and quickly concluded his remarks.

Closing arguments wrapped up on the morning of Tuesday, June 30. Judge Townshend announced a lunch break following which he would deliver his charge to the jury. *The Morning Chronicle*'s opinion of the charge would not have been encouraging to Wheeler, if he saw it: "The judge's address to the jury was most eloquent and impressive but against the prisoner." He first noted that at the supper hour on Monday "at the time when the murder was committed the prisoner was shown to be in the vicinity of the house, if not, indeed, in the house", confirming opportunity. He then addressed motive. "The learned judge commented on the motive that appeared to exist in the case and which, according to the testimony of witnesses, pointed strongly against the prisoner."

Inevitably, with Judge Townshend apparently joining the public in following the baying pack of newshounds being led along by Detective Power, at 5.10pm a guilty verdict followed after only two hours of deliberations. All concerned, excluding the unsuccessful Ruggles and the condemned Wheeler, would be free to enjoy the Dominion Day holiday on July 1. Overall, *The Digby Weekly Chronicle* wrapped up its coverage by concurring with Detective Power, reporting that the judge and jury, the press and the public gallery all agreed as to Wheeler's guilt. "The charge of the judge, though severe, was fully borne out by the evidence, and it was apparent the verdict of guilty was expected by the very large audience. When the verdict was delivered the expression was general that the evidence fully warranted the finding of the jury." And so Peter Wheeler came to find himself in the dark, musty room under the sheriff's front porch, and there he was strangled to death in the early morning hours of September 9, 1896.

The evidence against him was weak, certainly so weak as to introduce reasonable doubt. There were significant questions about the footprint evidence. More importantly, Power's timeline and hypothesis pointing to Peter Wheeler relied on categorically denying irrefutable forensic evidence. Dr Ellison placed the time of death in the early hours of Tuesday morning, not supper time on

Monday, as Power's timeline required. Dr Ellison was right. Power was guilty of bad detective work. His resolution of Annie Kempton's murder relied on questionable evidence and required that he disregard the best evidence, forensic evidence, that was understood at the time, indeed had been appreciated for centuries, and remains true today.

Unverified bloodstains on Wheeler's clothes proved nothing. Their origin was indeterminate. Further, animal blood would have been found on the clothes of almost any rural Nova Scotian who supplemented his diet by hunting and trapping which, in the 19th century, would have been a majority. Altogether not much by way of proof.

The footprint evidence was equally unreliable. First, Power's assertion 'I found no marks in the immediate vicinity other than those I have spoken of' was a bald-faced lie. At least one witness at the coroner's inquest testified that he had walked from the house to the barn shortly after the body was discovered. Another witness testified he had directed the detective's attention to the footprints after following them himself. A third testified he had walked to the barn when he heard the Kempton's cow lowing, needing to be milked. At the time there was no concept of crime scene management. Locking down the crime scene and setting up a perimeter to prevent contamination of the scene was unheard of. Quite the opposite was true. Acquaintances, neighbours, gawkers and amateur sleuths tramped across the yard, even through the house, for two days. A solitary set of footprints was a ridiculous claim.

It had even snowed again before Power conducted his investigation. Regarding the inconvenient snowfall Power told the court he simply wiped away the new snow! Further, snow is elastic, so over two days of variable temperatures and sunlight the footprints would have distorted in unpredictable ways. Power may have been 'on the scene at daylight and made a careful investigation' but his chronicler neglects to mention that it was dawn, days after the crime. The footprint evidence was unreliable. It was not best evidence, it was bad evidence.

Additionally, larrigans were a universal and generic type of footwear in rural Nova Scotia in the 19th century. Derived from traditional indigenous moccasins they had a leather sole with no distinctive tread or distinguishing features. The footprints may well have fit Peter Wheeler's larrigans. It was a good bet considering that innumerable pairs of larrigans in the neighbourhood would have roughly matched the misshapen footprints. The footprint evidence that Power dwelt on while he testified was not conclusive proof of Wheeler's guilt but rather, evidence of Power's slipshod and unscientific investigative work. Throughout his testimony his primary concern was fitting the facts and physical evidence to his narrative: typical of a bad detective.

Dr Ellison's calculation of time of death was scientific fact and no opinion, no matter how bullishly held and how loudly trumpeted, could override it. Power's narrative and Wheeler's movements demanded a supper time murder. That was the only time that he had the opportunity. Between that time and his discovery of the body on Tuesday morning he was with other people and had an alibi or he had been asleep in the boarding house. He did not have his own room, he slept in a small nook behind the kitchen stove. Multiple witnesses testified that he could not have left the boarding house during the early morning hours when the murder was committed without disturbing at least one of the other residents.

Moreover, Dr Ellison's estimate of time of death was irrefutable and accurate, based, as it was, on the three sisters—*algor mortis*, *livor mortis* and *rigor mortis*. Temperature, lividity and rigidity indicate time of death and they are subject to neither confusion nor opinion. Dr Ellison's assertion of the time of death was accurate and irrefutable. Dr Lovett's conclusion that Annie died "between the hour of 5 in the afternoon of Monday, the 27th day of January, and the hour of 8 o'clock in the morning of Tuesday, 28th day of January", allowed for Detective Power's timeline, but it flew in the face of widely accepted forensic evidence. It was as unjustified as his outrageous conclusion that Peter Wheeler was the likely culprit.

The *mortis* sisters cannot tell a lie. *Algor mortis* relates to the decline in body temperature following death. A cadaver cools at a rate of approximately 1° per hour, after cooling 2° in the first hour, as it drops to ambient temperature. This had been an established medical fact since mid-century. *Livor mortis* describes the manner in which blood pools in the lower parts of the body, creating distinct purplish discolouration like a severe bruise after death. The best known of the sisters, *rigor mortis*, involves the stiffening of the joints and muscles of a body a few hours after death, and their subsequent relaxation. The muscles stiffen, and relax, progressively beginning with the smallest in the face, hands and feet. Contraction of the iris muscles also dilates the pupils during *rigor mortis*. The phenomenon of *rigor mortis* was first described in 1811 by the French physician P H Nysten, although its physiological basis was not determined until the middle of the 20th century. Extreme cold, immersion and the physical characteristics of the deceased (a tiny infant as compared to an obese adult) can alter the timeline for the triumverate somewhat.

Knowledge of the evolution of the cadaver post-mortem was well understood in 1896. It required no specialised forensic techniques or advanced scientific equipment, but familiarity with the *mortis* sisters was essential. Dr Ellison had practiced for almost four decades and had well-earned experience with death. He knew the three sisters intimately. His estimate of time of death—probably 2am, not earlier than midnight and not later than 4am was accurate. It was based on observations well understood at the time and not contradicted in the 125 years since. Simply put, Annie Kempton died at a time that Peter Wheeler could not have killed her. She died at a time that absolutely refutes Power's theory. Undeniable physical evidence makes Power's timeline categorically impossible: Annie Kempton died in the early morning hours of Tuesday, not Monday evening as Power surmised, and Wheeler had no opportunity to commit the murder if it occurred on Tuesday morning. Peter Wheeler was an innocent man and Detective Power's reconstruction of the crime flew in the face of the facts. It required dismissing contradictory evidence and twisting any mildly implicatory evidence into conclusive proof of guilt beyond reasonable doubt. In plain terms, Peter Wheeler's execution was a grievous miscarriage of justice. A miscarriage of justice that followed from Power's bad detective work. He jumped to an *a priori* resolution of the case and then broadcast it early and often through ever-willing yellow journalists.

Perhaps Power really believed in his impossible theory and Peter Wheeler's guilt. Perhaps he could spot an easy target when he saw one. Perhaps he was persuaded initially by prosecutor Owen during their first case conference upon his arrival and too obstinate to subsequently acknowledge his rushed and wrongful error. The answer will never be known. Not a single instance of Detective Nicholas Power's handwriting exists. No diaries or letters to reveal his inner thoughts, no documents relating to his investigations, not even a signature on a receipt. What we do know is that Peter Wheeler could not have murdered Annie Kempton in the early morning hours of Tuesday, January 28, 1896, her established time of death.

The extensive coverage of the crime in every newspaper in the province from the day the body was discovered made selection of an untainted jury all but impossible even though a minor change of venue was granted. The trial, a foregone conclusion, was little more than a segue to the execution. Power, the press and the public had all convicted Peter Wheeler long before the stove pipe fell in Kentville's temporary palace of justice. Power's delight in presenting his theories as fact via the newspapers immediately upon his assignment to an investigation is common to Peter Wheeler and the plot against the Prince. In both instances Power rushed to publicise his narrative and, on both occasions, he was wrong, dead wrong in Peter's Wheeler's case. Breckton and Holmes survived their ordeal at Power's hands. The hysteria around the alleged Fenian conspiracy had evaporated by the time they were tried and Power's fantasies only cost the pair one year of their lives. But Power's relentless efforts to demonstrate Peter Wheeler's guilt, his tenacious pursuit of a conviction and his obstinate dismissal of confounding evidence cost an innocent man his life. He placed greater importance on his public profile, his image of always being right, than poor Peter Wheeler's life.

Power subverted the legal system. He placed his newspaper image of superior detecting skills, indeed infallibility, above the evidence, the truth and justice. Even more destructively, he manipulated the newspapers to try the case on their pages and in the public mind long before the scales of justice weighed-in. Peter Wheeler was condemned before he stood in Justice Townshend's court six months after he discovered the lifeless body of Annie Kempton. Nic Power was a bad detective because his image was more important to him than the integrity of the criminal justice system. Nic Power was a bad detective because he subverted the legal system by trying the case in the press before the trial. Nic Power was a bad detective because he orchestrated the conviction and death sentence that cost Wheeler, an innocent man, his life.

Peter Wheeler's irrefutable innocence raises a final, uncomfortable question. Since Peter Wheeler could not have murdered Annie Kempton, a person or persons unknown must have committed the crime. And they escaped punishment because of Detective Nic Power's obsession with pinning the blame on Peter Wheeler.

While Peter Wheeler awaited his fate, Detective Power soon found himself engaged in another capital case, a multiple murder. It was an investigation with international implications that continues to reverberate, although not in a manner complimentary to the scientific detective's reputation. The sensational nature of the crime quickly knocked Peter Wheeler off of the front pages and out of popular notice.

CHAPTER SEVEN

Bram

JULY 21, 1896 was an unpleasant day in Halifax. Almost three-quarters of an inch of rain fell, it was foggy, and the mercury did not make 70°. Hardly an ideal summer day, even in Halifax. It was weather befitting the arrival of the *Herbert Fuller*, a barquentine. It had spent the day before with the hook down unable to make The Narrows in the dense fog. This dismal morning at 6am local pilot William White was navigating the ship into port. The Stars and Stripes flew at half-mast indicating deaths at sea. Beneath it, erroneously, a tattered black flag signalled there had been a mutiny aboard. Her jolly boat followed, being towed behind.

She had left Boston's Long Wharf 18 days earlier, her hold full and deck piled high with 700,000 linear feet of lumber, bound for Rosário, a major port in Argentina, 300km up the Paraná River from the capital, Buenos Aires. There had been 12 on board including the captain, his wife, the two mates and a passenger. Now there were only nine, and at least one of them was a murderer. In the tarred canvas-covered jolly boat trailing, their battered heads wrapped in towels, shrouds improvised from bed sheets, lay the decomposing bodies of Captain Charles Nash, his wife Laura and the second mate, August Blomburg. All three were badly beaten and bloodied a week earlier by both the blade and the butt of an axe in the early hours of Tuesday, July 14, 1896. The frenzied killer had cleaved and crushed their skulls with such fury that the white walls were covered in gore, the bedding soaked in blood. Deep cuts in the overhead beams revealed that the attacker, in his mania, had hit the ceiling while swinging the weapon wildly.

Initially, the corpses had been stored in the jolly boat on the roof of the fo'c'sle. The rank odour of putrefying flesh had forced the jolly boat's removal. Preparing to haul it, a kink in the towrope threatened to snap the line, causing a momentary panic. Surviving First Officer Thomas Bram had the wheel placed in becketts—tied in place to hold the ship's heading—and all hands hauled the dinghy and its fetid cargo in and straightened the tow rope.

The death ship, small mercy, was an exceptionally beautiful bier. "A fine example of the East Coast barkentines which were commonly employed toward the end of the century in both coastwise and deep-water trades, especially to the Caribbean and the River Plate," according to maritime historian W F Bunting. Distinctively, she was "fitted with main and mizzenmasts of equal height, connected by a spring stay... [and] a proper gaff-headed spanker." The wheel was located centrally, abaft of the aft house. The aft house's central dining area boasted a lantern, clock, small stove and dining table. Surrounding it were cabins for the two mates, more commodious cabins for the captain and his wife, and a chart room. A lavatory, pantry and storage closet completed the accommodations.

Companion ways led fore and aft. The after-companion way, reserved for the captain and his wife, exited to the port side of the wheel and the deck was clear. There was a small curtained window in the starboard side of the aft house's stern wall. The forward companion way exited mid-ship, aft of the mizzen mast. Permanent steps segued into a second, improvised staircase to the top of the deck load. The six sailors lived communally in the fo'c'sle and would never have dared enter the aft house. The fo'c'sle also included a small cabin for the steward, Jonathan Spencer, and a small galley for his daily cooking.

The aft house was particularly cramped, and sleeping arrangements improvised, because it was uncommonly crowded. The *Herbert Fuller* had also aboard on this trip a passenger, an affluent, mildly unhealthy and wildly unsuccessful Harvard sophomore, Lester Hawthorne Monks. Completing his second year at Harvard without bothering to write his final exams, his transcript consisted of a fistful of Es (a hair above an F, not a contraction of excellent). Complaining of various respiratory and sinus ailments, Monks' doctor had recommended a sea voyage "to harden his constitution" according to *The Herald*. His father concurred and suggested that his son follow it with a year in Europe. Consequently, Laura Nash occupied her usual cabin, but Monks was decamped in the captain's cabin and the captain was bunking on the lounge on the starboard wall of the chart room.

There are intimations that dipsomania was at the root of Monks' academic challenges. His father may have felt that a long sea voyage would impose an enforced period of abstinence, a common 'cure' in the late-19th century. If this were the case, the attempt failed. Monks included in his luggage, dozens of bottles of brandy and whiskey, alongside 60 bottles of beer.

Captain Charles I Nash had been born into a shipbuilding and seafaring family in Washington County, Maine, 50 miles southwest of the border with New Brunswick. His father Alonzo's yard built the *Herbert Fuller* and his younger brother Wilbur, widely known as Willie, was captain of the barque *Elmita*. After a long courtship, most of which Nash spent absent at sea, he married 22-year-old Laura Agnes Ray, in May 1880. She was the daughter of sea captain A Judson Ray.

The couple were leading members of New England's seafaring elite, their hometown churning out a wooden ship a year throughout the late Victorian era. Unusually, but befitting both her birthright and her betrothal, the bride to be proposed to live aboard with the groom. To that end the aft house had been decorated sumptuously by shipboard standards and the captain had personally overseen the *Fuller*'s construction. The *Herald* correspondent lavished praise on its appointments: "There was nothing about that cabin to jar upon sensitive and cultivated tastes... The horizontal strips above the doors was [*sic*] stained a rich cherry, and here and there a conventional design, done in gold and blue, was to be seen." Together, the couple shared the freedom, ocean winds and adventure of the open sea for years together, until murder afloat ended their lives.

The first mate, Thomas Bram, was born in St Kitts, and of indeterminate ethnicity. He claimed a British mother and a 'Hollander' father. He was also reputed to have said that a sensible man would lie about his ancestry if doing so were beneficial. His birthdate is clear, 1864. At 12 he was crewing coastal traders and three years later he took ship for New York aboard the schooner *James A Brown*. Arriving in 1879 he became a naturalised citizen in 1888, marrying along the way. His captains spoke highly of his skill and diligence, as did his employer for almost three years, the New York Lighter and Transportation Company for whom he captained tugs and barges in New York City. His supervisor there, H L Joyce, described him as "an unusually competent man, having led a seafaring life for many years... He was bright and intelligent and scrupulously neat and well dressed—he was, in fact, away above the average river man." He went on to add: "I do not hesitate to say that had he come to me at any time before this affair, I would have given him his old position back."

He was also apparently an unusually devout Christian, and his religiosity was no death's bed epiphany. Years before the *Herbert Fuller* tragedy he had waited tables between turns at sea, and as with his maritime career, he was noticed by his employer, and promoted. Importantly, he was employed, even valued by the Dennett's restaurant chain, noted for its religiosity. They did not serve alcohol and the walls were decorated with biblical quotations. As he swung between service at sea and at table, his bifurcated nature also allowed for bursts of religiosity to alternate with wine, women and song.

In this regard he was also viewed as slightly touched or 'odd' by many of his companions and co-workers. The laudatory Joyce also remarked that "many people used to think that he was demented". A co-worker in one of the Dennett's restaurants recalled: "He always seemed queer—I can't tell you just how but he was queer." Clearly, Bram was an outsider. Socially, culturally and ethnically, he was an 'other', easily scapegoated.

As first mate, Bram had the run of the ship. He would later testify that he spent the crucial early hours of Tuesday, July 14, when the murders were committed, sitting and strolling atop the deck load amidships. His attention was directed to the leeward, for approaching ships that had the right of way, he would later testify. He certainly had the opportunity to commit the murder. However, he was not the only possible suspect. Sailor Francis M 'Frank' Loheac had been on watch atop the fo'c'sle and was clearly innocent. Four of the sailors and the steward, off duty and together in the fo'c'sle, shared a mutual, irrefutable alibi. The sixth sailor, helmsman Charley Brown, had been at the wheel astern of the aft house. He could have slipped down the aft companion way and committed the horrible slaughter. Most curious of all, Monks was in his cabin in the aft house throughout the assaults. He was closest to the victims and, as the only surviving occupant of the aft house might have become a victim himself. Alternatively, being in the aft house, he certainly had the opportunity to commit the murders. He would later confess to being awakened by Mrs Nash's scream, but hesitated to react. The first mate, the helmsman and the passenger—Bram, Brown and Monks—were the only possible suspects.

The crime was the story of the day in the local Halifax newspapers and despite their proximity they were wildly inaccurate. The *Herald* labelled the sensational crime "A Carnival of Murder on the High Seas". The *Herald* story erroneously identified the primary suspect as First Mate Brain and one of the victims, the second mate, as Blandberg not Blomburg. As ever in the era, speed, the elusive, exclusive 'scoop' was infinitely more important than accuracy. The following day, Thursday, July 24, the enormity of the calamity had grown. Under the headline, "GREATEST OCEAN TRAGEDY OF MODERN TIMES," *The Herald* lamented, "it seems scarcely possible to believe that such a ghastly drama could be enacted upon the Atlantic in this enlightened period." And apparently the use of all caps to indicate shouting and significance is not an invention of the Twitter generation.

Truth be told, while all aboard were incarcerated pending an investigation, only one had been interviewed and autopsies had yet to be completed. It would be generous to suggest that these stories were based solely on rumour and more honest to characterise them as speculation, even fiction. They had no basis in fact, but rather, were based on informed opinion, the informed opinion of the infallible Detective Power. By this point in his career Power's opinion was as good, even better, than the facts. The *Herald* asserted that Brown had seen Bram commit the murder and "Detective Power and others who heard Brown's statement remarked that the consul and others were much impressed with the straightforwardness. Brown answering freely the questions put to him." This is a smoking gun, knowing Power's *modus operandi*, he was playing his journalistic violin with vigour and virtuosity.

The coverage amply illustrates the hysterical popularity of crime news and the wide reach of Power's media image. The reports also reveal newspapers' willingness to present rumour as fact and, along with the bad detective, rush to judgement. It all adds up to a strong dose of Victorian fake news. Power seemed only concerned that he was at centrestage.

Remarkably, speaking to the significance of Halifax's recent connection to the growing national telegraph network, the story appeared in the 'Last Edition' of *The Evening Star* [Toronto] on July 21, the day the *Herbert Fuller* arrived in port. Apparently favouring velocity over veracity, the *Star* reported "there had been a mutiny on board". Considering the black flag, it was an understandable error. However, it then invented and embellished extensively. It identified two possible motives, robbery and plans to sell the cargo to Cuban rebels with the spoils divided amongst the mutinous crew. Debating motives for a non-existent mutiny is hardly journalism.

It reported first mate Thomas Bram was the murderer. "The evidence points to deliberate murder by the first mate." With no hesitation it contradicted itself, on the same page in a companion article proclaiming "the sailor at the wheel, astern of the aft house, Charley Brown" had confessed. The contradictory claims appeared on the front page above the fold, under the largest, lurid headline, 'Chopped to Pieces in the Ships Berths'. Hours later a story appeared on the front page of *The Globe*

[Toronto] asserting, simply and falsely "the First Mate charged with murder." No one had yet been charged and the investigation was barely underway.

On the day that the *Herbert Fuller* sailed into Halifax, *The Boston Daily Globe* published an extra, late edition headlined "TRIPLE MURDER AT SEA. Fearful Crime Committed on Vessel That Sailed from Boston". Three days later, on Friday, July 24, the *Halifax Daily Mail* noted that the "thrill of horror... has expanded to the neighbouring republic." This was not surprising as she had sailed from Boston, the victims were American, as were the limited pool of potential perpetrators, and it was an US-registered vessel.

As Consul General at Halifax, Darius H Ingraham, a former mayor of Portland, Maine was occupied with pedestrian matters of trade and routine processing of immigrants landing at Halifax, proceeding by train to the US. A triple murder of US citizens, with US citizens suspected, occurring aboard a US vessel was a tempest in an otherwise staid posting. Halifax had not seen such excitement since the diplomatic incidents that marked British-US relations during the Civil War 30 years earlier. Additionally, he may have known, and certainly knew of, the Nash and Ray families, as all were members of Maine's small coastal, commercial elite. He was determined to play a role in the proceedings. He immediately requested that the survivors be taken into custody, the ship secured by the Halifax Police Department and the putrid remains conveyed to the city morgue. The Halifax police were also required to document the crime scene, including gruesome photographs of the bloody aft house cabins. Finally, he wired Washington for instructions, promptly receiving a reply ordering him to assert US jurisdiction, an assertion that the Halifax authorities acceded to.

The *Herbert Fuller* was moored 100 yards off Market Wharf, at the foot of George Street. The government cutter *Argus* conveyed the survivors to Queen's Wharf from whence they were marched up Duke Street to the new city hall. Designed by Edward Elliot and completed in 1890, the cream and red sandstone building features granite construction on the ground floor and in the tower. The seven-storey tower has clock faces on the north and south sides. Today, the north face remains fixed at four minutes past nine to commemorate the Halifax Explosion of 1917. The police station was located in the basement of this public edifice and the Fullermen, so labeled by the newsmen, were all locked in the cells and ordered held *incommunicado*. Regardless, reporters would periodically gain access to them throughout their brief stay in Halifax. Furthermore, their cells were aligned in two rows facing a central corridor and it seems quite likely that they were able to communicate although they were incarcerated in individual cells.

All except Monks. He was installed in Chief O'Sullivan's office suite, also in the basement, but more commodious than the stone-walled, barred, barren cells. He was also permitted to send an urgent telegram to his father, 'SHIP IN HALIFAX COME AT ONCE' and he did, accompanied by his brother, Dr George H Monks. On the same train also was Captain Nash's brother, Captain Wilbur S Nash and John Swann of Swann & Son of New York, the ship's agents and part owners of the *Herbert Fuller*. The Nash party was booked into the Queen Hotel on Hollis Street, one of Halifax's finest hostelries, only a few doors north of the Halifax Hotel, for half a century Halifax's best. The elder Nash had already retained lawyer Frank G Forbes of Pearson, Forbes & Covert as local counsel.

At noon the *Argus* returned to the *Herbert Fuller*. Aboard Captain Stewart's cutter were three constables to secure the ship, Detective Power to investigate the scene of the crime, and the medical examiner, Dr Finn, to deal with the corpses. Again, Detective Power was at the centre of a case that was already generating attention across Canada and south of the border in New England. Meanwhile, 50 miles northwest in the Kentville jail, all but forgotten by the newshounds and public caught up in the latest nightmarish carnival of mayhem, Peter Wheeler stoically waited for Sheriff Benjamin Van Blarcom to 'jerk 'im up'.

On Dr Finn's order the jolly boat containing the victims was towed to Market Wharf. The bodies were then loaded into a hearse and the carriage proceeded up Prince Street to Argyle Street, the location of Snow & Co undertakers' establishment. A huge crowd greeted the bodies at the wharf, accompanied the hearse to the undertakers and, jostling and banging at the doors, spent hours filing past the hideous spectacles despite, a Snow employee later noted, "the decomposition and stench, frightfully mutilated". Some, fainting and screaming, overcome by the sight and the rank odour, had to be helped out.

This is hardly surprising. The skulls of the bodies had been crushed and cleaved and they had decomposed for a week. The tarred canvas would have protected the cadavers from avian predation but insect activity would have led to maggots beginning to liquify the soft tissue. According to forensic chemist, Dr Shari Forbes, director of the Secure Site for Research in Thanatology (decomposition), also known as the 'Death Farm' in Bécancour, Quebec, the bodies would be in the active decay stage. "The smell would be like ammonia (produced by maggots) as well as hydrogen sulphide [rotten eggs], so very pungent... and the odour would have been detectable quite a distance from the bodies, potentially several hundred metres away if there was even a small amount of wind on the day." That Haligonians would endure this wretched stench to view mouldering cadavers speaks volumes of their era's obsession with death, murder and mayhem.

In the evening, public curiosity slaked, the bodies were transported to the city morgue. Loaded into a hearse again, they were carried two blocks up the hill toward the

Citadel. Just shy of the fortress the hearse paused outside a four-storey red brick building built a decade earlier. The coffins were unloaded, hauled through an over-wide wooden door set back in the wall into the basement, and into the city morgue, the domain of medical examiner Dr William D Finn. His autopsy report would establish the cause of death for Stipendiary Magistrate George H Fielding's inquiry, scheduled to begin at 11am on the morning of Thursday, July 23.

First, understood but unspoken, young Monks had to be dealt with. Despite his social standing he was the only person known to have been in the aft house, the scene of the crime, at the time the murders were committed. If he was not the murderer, he was the only survivor, the other three occupants at the time dead. This is not to suggest that Monks was the murderer. Evidence indicates that he lacked the bodily strength, let alone the constitution, to commit such violent, physical assaults. He admitted that he heard Laura Nash scream twice, yet did not immediately go to her aid, but rather remained, cowering, in his cabin. Perhaps he was stuporous with drink. A published line drawing of Monks depicts a weak-chinned, pointy-nosed milquetoast, neither a hero nor a murderer. Regardless, his social standing and his family's economic weight made his exoneration the first order of business.

To this end, Fielding's inquiry was delayed, to allow Ingraham to deal with Monks. In Peter Wheeler's case the coroner's inquest began within hours of the body being discovered. In this instance, diplomatic issues and social niceties had to be cleared up first. The next morning the crowds surrounding the courtroom pressing to get one of the few seats were disappointed to hear Police Chief O'Sullivan announce that Fielding's inquiry was a non-starter until Consul General Ingraham's interviews were completed in another, undisclosed room. In that room Lester Hawthorne Monks was lawyered up and well represented by two affluent and influential family members and his local solicitor. Wilbur Nash and John Snow were also present. It was quickly determined that Monks would not be charged, and that he could be released on bail with a simple promise to appear as a witness at the trial. The unfortunate sailors, known for their peripatetic lifestyles, were all held in custody until the trial was completed, although they were mere witnesses facing no charges. With this detail wrapped up, Stipendiary Magistrate Fielding's inquiry could begin.

However, the magistrate was closing the barn door, to twist an old saw, after the horse had returned. In the days between the *Herbert Fuller*'s arrival and the magistrate's inquiry, Power, O'Sullivan and Ingraham interviewed the principals and reached their own conclusions. Power believed he had already solved the case. Ultimately, the magistrate's inquiry would amount to little more than a rubber stamp on Power's ratiocination. Having dispatched Monks, Power and O'Sullivan interviewed the helmsman,

Charley Brown. He told them that, through the small window in the stern wall of the aft house, he had seen Bram striking the captain with the axe. The die was cast. Power was convinced that Brown was telling the truth. Brown had seen Bram attacking the captain. Power had an eyewitness.

Accepting the Swede Charley Brown's story at face value, literally, Detective Power seized the initiative and undertook to interview Thomas Bram. He did so alone, there were no witnesses and no written record, only Power's testimony as to their conversation. Almost a foot taller than Bram and half again his weight, the detective's bulk filled the small office. Looming over the prisoner he started: "Bram we are trying to unravel this horrible mystery here. Your position is rather an awkward one. I have had Brown in this office, and he made a statement that he saw you do the murder."

Power explained Brown had been at the wheel and saw Bram attack the captain through the window in the stern wall of the aft house. Bram replied: "He could not have seen me from there."

Detective Power saw in this short response an implicit admission of guilt. In a case of garbled syntax rather than sleuthing excellence, Power took Bram's response to mean 'I did it, but I could not have been seen to do it from the wheel'. This requires a considerable leap of faith from a statement that could as plausibly mean simply one cannot see through the window into the chart room from the wheel. With self-confidence overruling investigation, Power declared the case solved to his satisfaction. To his mind his interviews had secured eyewitness testimony from Charley Brown and a confession from the murderer, first mate Thomas Bram, merely what one would expect from Canada's real-life Sherlock Holmes.

The *Herald* matched the certainty of Detective Power. By July 24, three days after the death ship arrived, the *Herald* had branded the now accurately identified first mate Thomas Bram as the murderer. It reprinted an article written by Thomas F Anderson, in Halifax reporting for the *Globe* [Boston]. "It is undoubtedly true not only that Bram is a man of quick uncontrollable impulse, but that he is imbued with a fanatical bent of mind on certain subjects, any one of which would be of a sufficiently strong motive for the commission of the crimes under the stated mental conditions." The newspapers were uncritically reproducing Power's reconstruction of the crimes and identification of the perpetrator as established fact.

Despite the palaver the *Herald*, while sniffing after any fact or fiction that it could print, no matter how prurient, sanctimoniously criticised the very public who read it for those salacious details. The editor lamented: "The manner in which people struggled to get a look at the mutilated, decomposing bodies was revolting. Men, women and children repaired to Undertaker Snow's rooms until three or four hours before the bodies were removed to the morgue and the sightseers turned away.

It is estimated that several thousand gazed upon the revolting spectacle. May Halifax never have another such tragedy." The *Mail*, the most sensational of the Halifax newspapers, positively revelled in the carnage. It put together a multipage, illustrated feature on diverse acts of piracy and murder on the high seas from the *Saladin* mutiny to "The Last Man Hanged in Halifax the Negro Doucey". The multiple murders inspired riotous interest in Halifax and made international news.

While they condemned Bram, the newspapers all seized on the passenger, Lester Hawthorne Monks, affluent and upper-class, as the hero of the story. Bram, a humble sailor of a darker complexion and indeterminant ethnic origin, became Monk's doppelgänger, the fiendish dervish wielding the axe.

Boston reporter Anderson drew the contrast in stark, dog-whistle terms. He described Monks as "an exceedingly good-looking and frank-appearing young fellow, a typical Harvard man in talk and action. He was attired in a neat suit of a light pattern, wore low cut shoes, and puffed away on a cigarette..." Clearly, educated and upper class, the portrait places Monks above suspicion. The next day Anderson dismissed Bram. "He wore a dirty-looking woolen shirt, without collar. His hair was closely cut. Bram is a most powerful looking man and has certainly a bad-looking face. When on the stand he carefully guarded every answer made." The contrast could be no plainer. Monks is 'frank', Bram is 'guarded'.

Bram has a 'bad-looking face', while Monks is 'exceedingly good-looking'. Bram is 'dirty', Monks is 'neat'. Without touching on the question of legal culpability, of guilt or innocence, the contrast is stark. Whereas Monks is honest and open, Bram is devious and reticent.

Journalists were ably assisted by Monks himself, who willingly exaggerated everything from his imagined leadership role to his nautical skills. The steward, despite his central role in the drama, was largely dismissed initially, possibly because he was African-American. Indeed, when the case went to trial the prosecutor began his questioning of Spencer by apologising to the jury for Spencer's ethnicity. In his opening statement when Bram finally went to trial in Boston, District Attorney Sherman Hoar stated: "The Lord—unfortunately—does not give it into my hands to make the kind of witnesses we would like to produce here, but you will judge them as they appear." Hardly reassuring to a man of indeterminate ethnicity like Bram.

With no one yet charged with the murders, despite Detective Power's certitude as to Bram's guilt, the drama moved on to Boston. The Fullermen were loaded aboard the *Halifax* bound for Boston in the early hours of Sunday, July 26, in an effort to avoid the crowds that had marked their arrival. Shortly thereafter the *Herbert Fuller* also left Halifax, bound for Rosário, with its aft house scrubbed clean. With a new captain and crew its cargo was bound for its intended destination, its mercantile duties interrupted but not abandoned. On July 27 the Fullermen arrived in Boston, escorted by Halifax Police Constable Thomas Kline. Having made headlines for days, thousands crowded Lewis Wharf as the *Halifax* tied up. They were there to see the Ivy Leaguer that scribes dubbed 'the boy hero' and the heinous, madman that every newspaper reader knew was guilty, first mate Thomas Bram.

Recall, however, as the drama moved on to Boston, no one had yet been formally charged with the triple murder. Despite the assurance of the infallible Detective Power and the braying voice of unanimity in the newspapers, no one had yet been charged with a crime. The decision that the state of affairs fell under American jurisdiction ended all legal developments in Canada. Despite his position as Consul General, Ingraham had no legal authority to lay charges. Legal proceedings could only begin on American soil, in an American courtroom. For the Fullermen this would mean an increasingly long incarceration, there being two exceptions, one expected and the other unlikely.

The first to step off the *Halifax* in Boston were Monks and his father, who had accompanied him. It was a sunny day and some journalists saw a plucky young man in a summer suit. Others reported him haggard and drawn after his heroic ordeal. Throughout the voyage father and son had enjoyed a stateroom and the run of the ship, unlike the sailors who continued to be locked up. Now, a carriage carried father and son to the family home in tony Longwood, west of the city, young Monks a free man. He was obliged only to attend at trial when required as a witness. Spencer, the steward, was imprisoned initially, but eventually released when a mysterious, anonymous benefactor agreed to post his bail.

As to the others, Kline handed his prisoners over to Boston police captain Thomas Cain. Cuffed and loaded into a patrol wagon, they were transported to Police Station 1. That afternoon Bram and Brown were both charged with the murders; individually, not as co-conspirators. For Bram, this must have seemed nothing more than the expected. Convicted by Power and pilloried in the press, he must have seen it coming. However, Brown may very well have thought that he had slipped the noose, with his testimony in Halifax to the effect that he had seen the murder of Captain Nash. Despite being only witnesses, the remaining sailors were also all detained. Their detention was justified by their rootlessness and mobility. If so inclined they could simply take ship beyond American jurisdiction. Arguably, unable to practice their livelihood while waiting to testify they would have been indigent and unemployed; compelled to take ship not fleeing justice but driven by poverty and starvation. Regardless, for three months, until the grand jury convened, the Charles Street Jail would be their home.

Ironically, the jail, an imposing and impressive example of Boston granite classicism, is today a boutique hotel, arguably Boston's finest. At the time however, its inmates were subject to an extraordinarily harsh regimen, widely regarded as both reformist and reforming. Widely known as the Auburn system after the penitentiary in New York State that developed it in the 1820s (and introduced 'Old Sparky' to the US in 1890), silence was imposed at all times, even exchanging glances was punishable, and beyond working and eating prisoners were held in solitary confinement. All communal activity was highly regulated from work routines to marching in lockstep. Secret passageways allowed warders to covertly observe their charges, described as "wicked and depraved, capable of every atrocity, and ever plotting some means of violence and escape" by one. These were the conditions that the Fullermen endured. Monks, relaxing at Marblehead, with the bluebloods at the Corinthian Yacht Club, incorporated 1888, undoubtedly charmed the ladies and challenged the men with his tales of hardship and heroism that summer. Recall, that filling a similar if more gruesome role, cost the humbler John Radclive his job serving similar yachting types.

The next morning Bram and Brown made the short trip west, again, to the federal courthouse. Completed only five years earlier, it is a monumental granite edifice of great physical presence that speaks to the gravity of the deliberations that are conducted within. It continues to serve as a palace of justice today. The arched centre entrance, accented with a stone balustrade above and supported on console brackets, interrupts a symmetrical, heavily articulated 13-bay façade with a unique half basement and first floor of rock-faced ashlar. Today, with the addition of a two-storey mansard roof added in 1909 it continues to function as a courthouse, and home to the US' oldest law library.

Regardless of the august surroundings the proceedings were brief that day. Charley Brown had yet to obtain counsel. Bram was represented by James Edward Cotter. Cotter was being paid by parties unknown, although it was rumoured to be the principals of Shepard & Morse, owners of the *Fuller*'s cargo and long-time acquaintances, and occasional employers, of Bram. Cotter immediately requested a continuance until Friday, July 31.

The overflow crowds must have been disappointed by the brevity of the hearing. Only Monks, of course, and strangely, Frank Loheac, the sailor atop the fo'c'sle, were called to testify. A fascinating exchange speaks volumes about Monks' elevated status. Charley Brown's new attorney suggested: "If there is anything on which to hold Brown, then there is equally strong ground on which to hold this young man Monks." Realising, perhaps by the look on Commissioner Fiske's face, his *faux pas*, he quickly added, it would be "preposterous, your honor" to suggest that Monks could do so. Social status clearly played a role in the courtroom, to Monk's benefit and Bram's detriment.

That Charley Brown was represented by Frank Dewey Allen also raises some interesting questions. Dewey was a politician and lawyer of considerable note, yet there is no indication as to how he became involved in the case, even if only briefly. A Republican, born in 1850, he was a member of the Massachusetts state House of Representatives from 1881-82, the Massachusetts Governor's Council from 1886-88 and US Attorney for Massachusetts for 1890-93. It is unclear whether he was acting *pro bono* or if Brown, like Spencer, had an anonymous benefactor. Subsequently, it would become moot when no charges were brought against Brown.

On October 20, a grand jury was called to order, again, in the federal courtroom. All the sailors were called to testify, along with a handful of other peripheral witnesses. As remains the case today, grand jury testimony is taken *in camera* and kept secret so nothing can be said of its discussions. The deliberations concluded the following day and its decision was soon circulating widely. According to *The New York Times* "The United States Grand Jury this afternoon reported an indictment against Thomas A Bram for the murder on the high seas of Capt. Nash, his wife, and second mate Blomberg." The following Friday, November 6, Bram was arraigned, formally charged and entered a plea of not guilty. Bram's lawyers requested "a continuance of the case in order to give them the opportunity to prepare arguments."

The trial opened on Tuesday, December 15, 1896. Bram was charged with only a single murder, that of Captain Nash. The prosecution had an eyewitness, Charley Brown, who stated he had seen, through the window in the aft house stern wall, the first mate attack the captain. Together with Bram's assertion before Detective Power that Brown could not have seen him, the prosecution felt certain that a conviction was guaranteed. Murder was a capital offence and convicted of one murder, or three, Bram was likely to hang so the prosecution chose to focus on the best evidence and a single count of murder. Notably, Charley Brown had made another transition, reverting from possible suspect to star witness. "His testimony, it is expected, will be most important in the trial of Mate Bram," *The New York Times* observed.

The stage had been set for this trial less than five years earlier, only 50 miles south of Boston. In the town of Fall River, the bodies of Andrew Jackson Borden, a wealthy manufacturer and developer, and his second wife, Abby, were discovered in their home (today, the house is a bed & breakfast[5]). Like the victims on the *Fuller*, they had been gashed multiple times with an axe or a hatchet. Outrageously, the principal suspect was their daughter, Lizzie, a 32-year-old spinster still living at home. The sensational trial, despite Lizzie's eventual acquittal,

---

5 Visitors who choose to stay in the 'John V. Morse Room' can sleep "in the room where Abby Borden was found murdered the morning of August 4, 1892, on the second floor. It was the room the uncle of Lizzie & Emma Borden had slept in the night before. Abby Borden was making up the bedroom after John Morse's unexpected overnight stay when she was brutally murdered."

attracted worldwide attention. Lizzie Borden had done for axes and local murders, what Jack the Ripper had done for Whitechapel during his rampage in 1888.

The trial was held in the US Circuit Court presided over by Justices Le Baron B Colt and the less memorably named Nathan Webb. The setting was, again, the Federal Building overlooking Pemberton Square. The building housed the Supreme Judicial Court, the Suffolk County Superior Court, the Boston Municipal Court and the Suffolk County Probate and Family Court. Delightfully, its stark exterior is in contrast to its bright, airy grand hall and richly-panelled courtrooms. It was in these august surroundings that Bram's life would hang in the balance.

The case was prosecuted by Sherman Hoar, heir to a long line of politicians and jurists in the Commonwealth of Massachusetts. Suffice to say his great-great-grandfather was a signatory to both the Declaration of Independence and the US Constitution, his uncle, George Frisbie Hoar, served as US Senator for Massachusetts for over a quarter of a century (1877-1904) and his cousin would go on to become a member of the Massachusetts legislature. All three were graduates of Harvard Law. In fact, strangely, while a student, Sherman Hoar was the model for the head of the John Harvard statue that still sits in Harvard Yard at his *alma mater*.

Bram was defended by James Edward Cotter, a skilled and dedicated attorney who could hardly claim the pedigree of his opponent. He had arrived from Ireland aged seven, in 1856. He had never been to any law school, let alone Harvard Law. He studied law with William B Gale, a Marlborough, Massachusetts attorney and was admitted to the bar on January 2, 1874. He subsequently made a name for himself representing numerous notorious defendants. Despite receiving only expenses from the DA's office, he was determined to ensure Bram had a fair trial by defending him to the best of his ability.

On an unseasonably warm Tuesday morning, five months to the day since the murders had occurred, the trial opened before Justices Colt and Webb and a jury selected the day before. Opening remarks by counsel, incidental witnesses and the inconsequential testimony of Lester Monks occupied the bulk of the first few days' proceedings. Despite the excitement that Monks' appearance on Thursday occasioned it offered nothing new nor of importance.

The week's fireworks were reserved for Friday, December 18, when Charley Brown took the stand. Hoar's first question set the tone, "Mr Brown, what is your real name?" "Justus Leopold Westerberg," he replied, going on to explain that an immigration officer in Quebec City had assigned it to him and it stuck.

Passing on, their key exchange focused on what he had seen through the aft house window while doing his trick at the wheel: "I saw him [Bram] lift a weapon—I could not say what kind of a weapon. It was; I saw the handle. It looked to be on an ax; it was a long handle. I saw a blow fall in the direction of the captain's head."

Cross-examination chipped away at Brown's story, until Cotter dropped his bombshell. He asked Westerberg about an earlier incident in Rotterdam; an incident in which he had attempted to shoot a man while apparently in the throes of paranoid delusions. Westerberg initially denied it. When pressed, his exculpation was a masterwork of doublespeak. He said he had been suffering from amnesia and did not remember the attack while confessing that he, of course, remembered that he had been *told* of the attack. However, the latter was not the question he had been asked! Despite this duplicity, Brown's testimony stood as offered: He had seen Bram commit the murders.

Hoar's next witness was intended to deliver the *coup de grâce*, testimony to a confession from an unimpeachable source, a police officer, and not just any police officer, the internationally renowned sleuth Detective Nicholas Power. More substantial than anyone else in the courtroom, the detective loomed large as he took his place on the witness stand. He testified that when he interviewed Bram in the days immediately after the *Fuller* arrived in Halifax, Bram had asserted that Brown could not have seen him commit the murders as he could not have seen him from his position at the wheel. Power inferred that Bram was arguing not that he was innocent, but rather that he could not have been seen committing the murders.

Cotter objected strenuously, arguing that the

confession, if it was one, was not freely given. He argued that Bram's rights had been violated when he was stripped and searched at some point prior to Power's interview. He also objected to Power's prefacing his interview with the statement that he had spoken to Charley Brown and already deduced that Bram was the culprit.

At this point Justice Webb intervened and addressed Detective Power directly: "You say there was no inducement to him in the way of promise or expectation of advantage?"

"Not any, your honour."

"Held out?"

"Not any, your honour," Power repeated.

"Nor anything said in the way of suggestion to him that he might suffer if he did not, that it might be worse for him?"

"No, sir. Not any."

"So far as you were concerned, it was entirely voluntary?"

"Voluntary, indeed," Power concluded, and his testimony was allowed to stand.

As an aside Power added that Bram's decision to throw the murder weapon overboard was evidence of his guilt, inspired by fear that his fingermarks (known today as fingerprints) would have been found on the axe handle. While not essential to this case, his comment offers insight into Detective Power's willingness to squeeze the evidence into his mould. Only six months earlier, during Peter Wheeler's trial, Power had testified that he neglected the bloody handprints and fingermarks on the walls and windowsill of Annie Kempton's house because they were not a proven and reliable method of identification. Suddenly, in Boston, fingermarks had become a reliable method of identification and fear of them led Bram to dispose of the murder weapon, implicit evidence of his guilt. Apparently, Power would say and do whatever it took to convict his chosen perpetrator. To his mind, evidence was admissible if it bolstered his narrative and, otherwise, inadmissible.

He was willing to ignore any evidence that undermined his reconstruction of the crime. In Peter Wheeler's case, only weeks earlier, Power had ignored forensic evidence. His theory that the crime occurred early Monday evening was demolished by the three sisters, accepted and irrefutable forensic evidence that the murder had occurred in the early hours of Tuesday morning. Tenaciously, he imposed this narrative on the newspapers, the public, the jury and, fatally, Peter Wheeler. In this case Power held that Charley Brown could not have committed the murders because he could not have left the wheel without the *Herbert Fuller* straying off course. There are two significant problems with this belief. In multiple instances the trial record refutes this assertion. Numerous experienced sailors, including captains, introduced as witnesses by Cotter, testified that the wheel could be put in becketts and left for extended periods. This very action was undertaken when the jolly boat was being put astern and the line developed a kink. Detective Power's decision that Charley Brown was not the murderer hinged on him having no opportunity because he could not have left the wheel: a falsehood.

Moreover, if he had never left the wheel, he could not have seen the murder of Captain Nash. Diagrams of the cabin's layout introduced as evidence and a bizarre attempt by the jury to recreate the situation during their deliberations demonstrated that there was no sightline from the helmsman's position through the window into the chartroom. If Charley Brown had never left the wheel, he could not possibly have seen the murder. If he had seen the murder, he must have left the wheel, undermining his alibi that he had not had the opportunity because he could not have left the wheel. Detective Power's overweening self-confidence, his belief in his infallibility, allowed him to simply disregard this evidence. Ignoring contradictory evidence and a plausible suspect in single-minded pursuit of a conviction is execrable detective work: it was the bad detective's trademark. While often light on truth, his pertinacious resistance to contradictions and distractions and a tenacious focus on his chosen prey was Power's *modus operandi*. Neither truth nor justice, not even facts, were more important to Detective Power than his intuition and, even more so, the image of his infallible intuition.

The court had heard from an eyewitness, although Charley Brown's testimony was questionable on multiple grounds. If he was not an eyewitness, he was a suspect. Surely, reason enough to testify to another's guilt. Particularly when one had in the past had a fit of paranoia that resulted in attempted violence. Finally, he had lied to the court, opening up the possibility that the common law principle '*Falsus in uno, falsus in omnibus*' (a Latin phrase meaning 'false in one thing, false in everything') should come into play. In simplest terms, having been shown to lie in one instance—the attack of violent paranoia—all his testimony, specifically that he witnessed the attack, becomes unreliable. Regardless, Charley Brown's eyewitness testimony and Detective Power's confession were both included in the official record, evidence to be considered by the jury during their deliberations. With its two most important points established by witness testimony, the prosecution rested.

The next day the defence would commence and Cotter had let it be known that his first witness would be the accused, first mate Thomas Bram. In the public gallery, Charles E Grinell eagerly awaited Bram's testimony. Grinnell, a local barrister, was only an observer at this trial. He would later publish an article, "Why Thomas Bram was Found Guilty", in the legal journal *The Green Bag*.

Unfortunately, Bram's testimony proved an anti-climax. He detailed his movements throughout the fatal night. He admitted to having taken a drink or two, but insisted he was not impaired. Most importantly, he repeatedly denied that he had committed the murders, nor had any knowledge of who had committed them, although he remarked that Julius Westerberg, aka Charley Brown, was an obvious candidate.

A humourous exchange during Hoar's cross-examination revealed the lawyer's lack of sailing knowledge and that Bram retained his sense of humour despite his circumstances.

"Were you in the longitude of Cayenne [French Guiana] when you changed the course on the day after the murders?"

"Yes, sir."

"And were you in the latitude of Cayenne also?"

"If we were, we would have been in Cayenne, sir."

On the other hand, Justice Cotter was an amateur yachtsman and knowledgeable sailor. He frequently interrupted Bram's testimony to discuss intricate details of seamanship in jargon that left most of the courtroom, not the least of which was Hoar, baffled.

Justice Webb read his charge to the jury on New Year's Day, 1897, and, unsurprisingly, a verdict of guilty was returned the following day. Media madness persisted. By January 3 his sentence was being covered as far afield as Florida where *The Florida-Times Union* (Jacksonville) reported, "Thomas Bram, mate of the barkentine Herbert Fuller was found guilty today of the murders committed on that vessel last July. The jury went out at 1.30pm yesterday. At 10 o'clock this morning they reported that they could not agree. Judge Colt directed them to retire for further consultation. They were again locked up, with the result that at 3.40pm they announced a verdict of guilty." Again, this obscure article serves to illustrate the popular obsession with murder and mayhem. Tragedy anywhere inspired coverage everywhere.

Sentencing was delayed, but it was a foregone conclusion, the verdict carried a compulsory death sentence. On March 9, 1897, Bram heard the fateful words, "You will be taken hence to the place of execution and there be hanged by the neck until you are dead. May God have infinite mercy on your soul." While New York State had introduced the electric chair in the summer of 1890, it would not be employed in Massachusetts until December 17, 1901, consequently, Thomas Bram had a date with the hangman. Cotter immediately appealed and Bram's case was scheduled to be heard by the Supreme Court in the fall when the justices returned from their circuits.

Cotter and co-counsel Asa Palmer French appeared before the justices on the afternoon of Monday, October 18, 1897. During the trial they had collected a list of 67 different causes of error that provided grounds for a new trial. However, they only had one hour in front of the court, so they had to focus on their strongest, most salient arguments. They targeted Detective Power's slipshod interrogation methods and documentation. French argued, "The whole aim and purpose of the examination and interview was to intimidate the prisoner and induce him to say something which would tend to incriminate him. In the interests of fairness and public justice, such inquisitorial methods should not be countenanced." He continued, "Testimony of this sort should be admitted with the greatest of caution when the prisoner and detective are alone. There must be no direct or implied inducement, however slight, and no exertion of any improper influence."

Two months later the high court ruled. The justices held, "That this statement made by the accused to a police officer, was evidently not a voluntary confession and was not admissible as evidence against him." It ordered, "The judgement is reversed, and the cause remanded, with directions to set aside the verdict and to order a new trial." The justices went beyond this simple order and, in their judgement, they excoriated Power, "A plainer violation as well of the letter as of the spirit and purpose of the constitutional immunity could scarcely be conceived of." The verdict was nullified, the trial invalidated and a new trial ordered on the basis of one point of law, Power's *in camera* interrogation of Bram was tainted by 'implied inducement, however slight' and 'exertion of any improper influence'. Power blew it. His unorthodox and illegal interrogation resulted in the verdict being overturned. This is a sterling illustration of bad detection. In Boston, Power took centre stage, pleased to be in the spotlight during the trial. Following Cotter's appeal Power retained the spotlight, but for his blunders, not his erudition. Needless to add, Power did not testify at Bram's second trial.

Unfortunately, Bram's new trial did not exonerate him and Power's malign influence continued to ruin his life. He was convicted again but avoided capital punishment, being given a life sentence.

In a bizarre twist befitting the strange links between fact and fiction, crime and imagination in this era it was a novel that finally freed Bram from Power's evil clutches. In 1914 Mary Roberts Rinehart, a popular writer of everything from novels and short stories to poetry and travelogues published her 10th novel, *The After House: A Story of Love, Mystery and a Private Yacht*. It was a highly fictionalised murder mystery loosely based on the *Herbert Fuller* tragedy. The *Fuller* had become the luxury yacht *Ella*. The protagonist is an amalgam of Spencer and Monks, an affluent Ivy Leaguer in search of excitement, serving as steward. The murderer is an eccentric sailor, a stand-in for Charley Brown. Despite the changed details the novel was widely known to be based on the *Fuller* tragedy. It reignited interest in the Bram conviction. According to the New England Historical Society, "Rinehart's books were extremely popular, and she had a fan in Teddy Roosevelt. Roosevelt took an interest in the case and bought Rinehart's version of events. He lobbied President Woodrow Wilson to pardon Bram." Bram was released from the federal penitentiary in Atlanta in 1913 and fully pardoned six years later. Finally, he achieved a lifelong dream of captaining his own ship when, in 1926, he became the co-owner of the *Alvena*.

Thomas Bram survived, barely, his encounter with Detective Nicholas Power. In that sense he came off better than the late Peter Wheeler, but nothing can change the fact that crossing paths with the bad detective cost him almost a quarter of a century, approximately one-third of his span on this mortal coil. His only offences seem to have been his ethnicity and complexion. In Detective Power's mind these were enough to convict him, and absolve a mentally disturbed European with a history of paranoid violence. Thomas Bram's life was turned upside down, and Charley Brown's protected, because Nicholas Power was a bad detective.

Ultimately, the Bram case presents a unique Catch-22 of ineffectual detection. If Bram was not the murderer, then Power's detective work had been misdirected. His laser focus on Bram allowed the murderer (presumably Brown/Westerburg) to escape unpunished: bad detective work. If Bram was the murderer, Power's sloppy interrogation technique allowed him to escape the noose on a technicality. Either way, Detective Nic Power's bad detective work in the *Herbert Fuller* affair did nothing but muddy the waters. It is a classic case of Catch-22. If Bram was guilty, Power's unorthodox methods undermined the prosecution of a multiple murderer—bad detective work. If Bram was innocent then Power played a driving role in framing an innocent. In either case, it was an abysmal performance by a bad detective. No matter how it is viewed, justice suffered for Power's performance.

CHAPTER EIGHT

The Last Decade (1896-1906)

On New Year's Day 1897, Detective Nicholas Power was on the top of his game in his mind, that of the press and popular opinion. Despite the abject and obvious falsity of his Fenian plot, it persisted in the public mind. Most recently, he had, again in the realm of perception, successfully concluded two headline-grabbing murder cases. The investigation into the murder of Annie Kempton had concluded successfully with the conviction and execution of Peter Wheeler. His death stood as proof of Detective Power's erudition. Wheeler's cold, dead corpse was a feather in Detective Power's broad blue hat band. As recently as 1989 Peter McGahan, Director of the Atlantic Institute of Criminology, wrote approvingly of Power's detective skills in the case and it is only in this century that Debra Komar has brought forward conclusive evidence of the impossibility of Wheeler's guilt. Then, a second trial reaffirmed Thomas Bram's guilt, despite Power's illegal interrogation resulting in his evidence being disallowed. While US courts might object to Power's methods the second conviction seemed to demonstrate that his conclusion that Bram was the murderer was correct. Both cases had garnered headlines across Canada and the US and accolades for the mountain of a man, with an ego to match, that was bad Detective Power.

Sherlock Holmes, with a perfect record of convenient, reassuring resolution of each case at the story's conclusion, was at the height of his fame and Detective Nicholas Power was Canada's Sherlock Holmes: every one of his investigations appeared to conclude with a conviction. During his final decade as a detective, Power repeatedly made the front pages, reinforcing his image of infallibility. With the benefit of hindsight, it is apparent that Power's reputation had a very shaky foundation and was constructed of straw. No amount of myth-making would rescue the bad detective from thoroughly botching his final murder investigation as a detective (and then his first investigation as chief when he was promoted).

In the fall of 1897 Detective Power was called to Windsor, Nova Scotia, at the junction of the Avon and St Croix

Rivers, 40 miles north west of Halifax. On Sunday, October 17 a fiery conflagration had ravaged the town's poorest quarters, leaving 500 families dispossessed, their houses, bedding and clothing incinerated. Three quarters of the population, 3,000 souls, were homeless. Total losses were eventually calculated to be $1,500,000. Detective Power was dispatched to investigate its cause. *The Globe* report is painfully revealing of the casual racism of the era: "It is still believed it was started in a negro dive, which was a resort for characters of the worst type." The 'negro dive' was later identified as a billiard room owned by "Fletcher, the colored man". A month after the fire, on November 15, George Fletcher was formally charged with arson.

In August 1900, with the Boxer Rebellion and the Boer War dominating the headlines, Detective Power pinched a Swedish murderer, Johan Hannu. After serving a 12-year prison sentence for nine murders, Hannu had been deported from Sweden. Landing in Scotland he had boarded a Leyland Frederick & Co steamer for Halifax, planning to head for Winnipeg. Power and Immigrant Agent Clay had him in handcuffs before he debarked from SS *Assyrian*.

Typically, in 1901 Detective Power repeatedly made appearances in newspapers across the country. On March 20, in Toronto, *The Globe* reported that he had captured Walter Pope, an embezzler who had fled England ensconced in a stateroom aboard the Allan Line's RMS *Corinthian*.

In May, a strange case that stymied Power, had his name in the news nationally nonetheless. On May 1, a lady signed the register of the elite Halifax Hotel as Mrs Mary D Eastman of Quebec. The next morning, she told the maid she felt unwell, attributing her illness to a salad she had consumed on the train trip the previous day, and requested a glass of wine. That afternoon she hired a cabman, Tom Fraser, and undertook a concerted search for a revolver. At Sarre's on George Street, a sporting goods store and tobacconist, she was told they did not carry firearms, but helpfully the clerk suggested Cragg Brothers & Co, at Barrington and George streets, only a few blocks away. They stocked firearms, but none suitable for a lady. Finally, she found what she wanted, a Harrington & Richardson revolver, at hardware and carriage goods merchant George E Smith & Co, on Bedford Row at Cheapside. Later that day Mrs Eastman was found in her room dead, the revolver on the floor, a fatal bullet wound in the right side of her head.

It was quickly determined that Eastman was an alias and Detective Power was charged with determining her identity. He discovered she had lunched in Amherst, Nova Scotia while aboard the train to Halifax. He also traced her to the Dufferin Hotel in St John, New Brunswick, where she registered as Mrs Mabel W Cross of Wolfeboro, New Hampshire. Despite tips and inquiries pouring in from across the continent the trail went cold. She was not an errant wife from New Hampshire, nor a music teacher from Sherbrooke, Quebec. Despite the newspaper attention to the suicide of a wealthy but anonymous woman, she was never identified. In contrast, Power was always identified in the news reports and that was the most important point to him. 'Any press is good press as long as they spell your name right' could have been his motto if it was not already the 'Man who saved the Prince'. Ironically, while the victim's name was never discovered, Power's was front and centre throughout the sensational newspaper coverage.

In the fall of 1901, on October 16, *The Herald* reported that Power had just returned from Clark's Harbour on Cape Sable Island, "investigating the Kaplan murder. He succeeded in obtaining a lot of valuable evidence. The detective had little rest during his trip and was rather fatigued on the return." The emphasis on his exertion and attention to his wellbeing testifies to his celebrity status.

Less than two weeks later *The Toronto Daily Star* was reporting on his arrest of A Harley. Harley, formerly manager of the Fredericton branch of the Bank of British North America was wanted for allegedly absconding with $6,000 belonging to "a gentleman from Scotland". Harley is described as "a good football player... a favourite in social circles." Significantly, in typical Halifax fashion, the perpetrator's social station was such that the disposition of the case would be unusual: "It is probable that the matter will be quietly arranged and there will be no prosecution." South side blue blood or Ivy League outsider, as had been the case with Lester Monks, Detective Power, and the department's leadership, served and protected the socio-economic elite, they did not prosecute them.

Throughout 1901 Detective Power repeatedly made the headlines and he kept it up into the New Year. On January 21 he rooted out a murderer who had been on the run for almost two years. In 1900 Walter Gordon murdered Jacob Smith and Charles Daw in Whitewater, Manitoba, a dozen miles north of the US border. He deposited the bodies in an old well. Gordon had contracted to buy Daw's farm as Daw planned to return to England to marry. Gordon moved into the farmhouse alongside Daw and Jacob Smith in July. On August 1, Daw was nowhere to be found and it was impossible to close the deal. It was assumed Daw was in Brandon bidding farewell to friends. By September locals were beginning to look askance at Gordon. When Daw's solicitor received a letter from concerned relatives in England, rumours became accusations. Gordon fled to Winnipeg and then vanished.

He crossed the border and enlisted in the US Army as John Gray of Buffalo, New York. Stationed at Fort Meade, North Dakota he deserted when he heard the Canadian Mounted Rifles were recruiting and bound for South Africa. It was trooper John Gray who eventually confessed to his true identity, that Detective Power arrested at the Rifles' military camp on the exhibition grounds. A tip and description from Winnipeg Police Chief Elliott put Power on to his prey.

Gordon was returned to Manitoba to stand trial. His Halifax Police Department escort, Constable Walter Hyndman, and his US Army immediate superior, a cook named John F Sears, both testified that he had confessed. Dr Gordon Bell testified to a family history of mental illness, including his mother's suicide and his brother's commitment to an asylum. He described the accused as "a raving maniac" and asked the court to have mercy. The jury disagreed and, after only a few hours' deliberation, they found Gordon criminally responsible and guilty. On June 20, 1902, at 8.04 in the morning he was dispatched by John Radcliffe, Canada's official executioner. Ticket-holders, limited to 150 spectators selected by Brandon Sheriff William Henderson, watched him drop and heard the snap as his vertebrae ripped apart. The story had little to do with Power beyond the arrest, but it was an arrest made by the 'Man who saved the Prince' and kept his name in the news throughout the first half of 1902.

In April 1904, Detective Power was assigned a nightmarish carnival of mayhem that must have been the strangest incident in his long career. The problem was a fire at the Queen Hotel. Three commercial travellers staying at the Halifax Hotel had walked up Hollis Street to visit a 'friend' staying at the Queen Hotel. Finding their friend absent, they entered his room and ransacked it. "The furniture was smashed and everything in the room was piled in disorder. The electrolier [an electric chandelier] had been torn down and placed under the bedclothes with the current turned on. The thing ignited…" When Detective Power attempted to arrest the trio the next day at the Halifax Hotel, *The Herald* reported: "Charles E Goatham of Montreal, a Jew… who is a big, powerful man, resisted arrest and started to 'do up' the detectives, but was badly treated, and driven to the police station in a battered condition." Even in his sixties, Detective Power could, and would, do it up. However, he would have been infuriated had he known the incident made *The Toronto Daily Star* but his name did not. Unfortunately, it was impossible to determine the final disposition of this case.

A month later, a contractor on the Halifax and South-Western Railway (terminus in Yarmouth) then under construction, had "one of the most valuable horses owned by him" stolen. A few weeks later Chief O'Sullivan received information that the horse had been sold at Rawdon Centre, Hants County, 35 miles north of Halifax. With the owner in tow to identify the mount, Detective Power was dispatched to investigate. He quickly located the horse, and the entirely innocent new owner, who considered it a great deal at $40, a veritable steal at that price. His description of the seller allowed Power to identify him as 'Sweeney', a notorious Halifax crook who had already seen the inside of Rockwood and Dorchester

Federal Penitentiary in New Brunswick. Learning he was working on his victim's railway construction contract, Power set off for the job site. Speaking to his fearsome reputation, *The Herald* correspondent reported that news of the great detective's arrival spread like wildfire and many men "struck for the woods" including Sweeney "who succeeded in getting away". Power, "a relentless pursuer," according to *The Herald*, eventually captured him. The clue is fascinating. Sweeney had fled without his coat and hat and, lacking those two items, even amongst farmers and labourers, he stood out like a sore thumb in 1904. Another notch in Power's belt and a stunning example of journalism's ongoing battle with accuracy (or a drunken typesetter) in this single story *The Herald* identifies the victim variously as Hurrett, Surrette and Surrett!

That fall Power wrapped up an investigation that echoes through the years. With the proliferation of online shopping the offence has reappeared and perpetrators are known as porch pirates—the thieves that steal packages delivering online purchases. The same scam, but different technology, was as popular a century ago as it is today. The bunco artist would place an order with a Halifax merchant from a nearby community, in this case, Birch Cove, a few miles north of Halifax. The order would be placed in the name of a local resident with an account with the merchant and never arrive, being intercepted by agents of the con man when the packages were dropped off at the train station. The victimised consignee would then be shocked to receive a bill for goods they had neither ordered nor received. After the scam had been successfully carried out repeatedly, in September 1904 a group of merchants approached Chief O'Sullivan with their concerns, specifically four suspicious orders to be delivered to Birch Cove that evening. Detective Power was assigned the case.

Power decided to have two of the orders filled. G M Smith and Co shipped sundry items from its store on Hollis Street and W Charles Anderson, family grocer on Granville Street, filled an order for sweets and treats including fruit, jellies, jams and raisins. With officers Kennedy and Hanrahan, Power planned to place the Birch Cove railway station under surveillance. Riding with the packages on the 6.30 suburban train, they slipped off it on the side opposite the station while the brakeman deposited the packages on the platform. Shortly, two teenage sisters, Hazel and Irene Gray, arrived and were arrested by the waiting sleuths. Another successful investigation, and one surely appreciated by the Southside swells whose commercial life was being disrupted.

In his final year as a detective, Power continued to make the headlines. In the spring of 1905 he nabbed a young Englishman preparing to flee Canada on an outbound steamer. Joseph Alexander had stolen a large amount of money from his employer in Lennoxville, Quebec and taken to his heels. A telegram from the police department there indicated he would make for

England from Halifax or St John, New Brunswick. Assigned the case Power took to greeting the *Maritime Express* each day as it arrived at the station. The *Maritime Express* was the Intercolonial Railway's flagship train, luxuriously transporting passengers directly from Montreal to Halifax daily. No expense was spared and, according to railway historian D N W Smith, the two drawing rooms in the first-class section were "finished in polished mahogany beautifully inlaid with lighter woods [with] ceilings of green and gold, in the Empire style." Power's diligence paid off on Monday, April 10. He engaged a likely looking passenger in conversation, learning his name was John Smith. Power saw through the paper-thin pseudonym and the man confessed to being Joseph Alexander, the wanted man.

Some hours later, Power's human package was wrapped in a bow. The detective was summoned to the S Cunard & Company offices on Upper Water Street. Alexander had indeed booked passage to England and the Cunard checker responsible for moving passengers' luggage from the train to the ship had picked up a grip from Alexander's seat. It was passed to Power and when he opened it he discovered paperwork, in French, belonging to a lawyer from Rimouski. Rimouski is over 250 miles from Lennoxville, but on the *Maritime Express*'s route to Halifax. It was determined that Alexander had stolen the bag from another passenger and he was charged with the second crime also.

In the summer of 1905 Power solved a difficult case that had bedevilled Halifax's mercantile elite since the spring. J P Fairbanks, proprietor of the Queen Hotel, first brought the matter to his attention in May. His guests were having problems with their mail. "Registered letters and letters containing cash had reached their destination minus the contents, and two had been sent back to him." The two returned letters had been readdressed by the same hand. Concurrently the postmaster had reported to Detective Power that bank and business mail boxes at the post office were being rifled.

A break in the investigation did not occur until late August with the report of a related offence. On Monday, August 28, 1905, R B Thomas, local agent for the Canadian and American Express companies, made the short walk from his office on Hollis Street to city hall. In the basement he asked to speak to Detective Power. Seated in his office he handed Power a $50 money order returned by the Canadian Express head office. It had been stolen from a hotel room, but the King Edward, not the Queen Hotel. He had with him a second one that his local teller had retained when a suspicious payee abandoned it and fled. Both were endorsed with the same signature, and it matched the envelopes Power had held since May.

Power headed north for the King Edward Hotel where he met with the talkative manager, Mr Wilson. Wilson told the detective that the hotel's porter, Joe

Lewis, had access to the room in question and that as the hotel messenger he made two trips to the post office daily. He added that Lewis spent lavishly on his lady friends and was altogether too 'sporty' and well dressed for one of his station and $20 monthly income. Suggestions that he was known to 'hobnob' with the night porter at the Queen Hotel further implicated Lewis. Power quickly arrested Lewis on Sackville Street and dragged him north up Hollis Street to the Canadian Express office at number 239. There the clerks, Mulcahy and Fultz, identified him as the party that had tried to cash the money order. With the arrest Power resolved multiple offences and problems for two of Halifax's finest hostelries. Needless to add, it kept his name on the front pages.

Also in September, Detective Power donned a disguise to investigate a report of 'indecent actions' on Citadel Hill. According to *The Herald*: "Officer Power went into the Central engine house and disguised himself as a fireman, with a rubber coat and hat, went up the town clock stairs and observed very unseemly conduct on the part of the trio." This incident reveals Power's creativity, commitment and also that he continued, at the height of his popularity, to participate in the minor and mundane matters of policing and social control. In 1905, interesting evidence of Detective Power's importance was also revealed by the police budget. In that year, for the first time, $25 was allocated to pay for a home telephone for Nic's residence. He was the only member of the department, other than Chief O'Sullivan, to be provided with the newfangled contraption.

Nic's last murder investigation was the pinnacle of his career as a bad detective, the height of his 'badness'. He managed to screw up on multiple levels while revealing a cold, heartless, self-righteous side. Thoroughly bad in every sense of the word. Detective Power's final capital case follows a painfully familiar script, made only more heinous by the nature of the crime, infanticide.

Plympton, Nova Scotia is located on the east coast of St Mary's Bay, only 15 miles west of Bear River. In 1905, home to three churches, a school and a post office, the community had just survived a hellish winter. From mid-February into March snow had stopped the trains and coal shortages had left the region shivering. The summer had been late coming and cool. Saturday, June 17 was a glorious exception with sunshine and the temperature reaching the nineties, but Plympton was labouring under a cloud. The night before two little girls, a toddler and a six-year-old, had disappeared, and it was feared they had been carried away by tramps.

On that hot Saturday afternoon, the community's worst fears were realised. Searchers numbering over two dozen had been at it through the night when local teenager Fred O'Neil came across the body of barely living toddler Ada Hope 'Elma' Young at one in the afternoon. An hour later, Fred's brother Clifford discovered the infant's six-year-old sister, Minnie Alice 'May' Young, not far away and sadly, dead. Needless to add, the horrible tragedy was fodder for the newspapers, and the story was instantly national news.

The Toronto Daily Star spared its readers none of the details. The infant "was lying on its face, trussed hand and foot, but alive. Its mouth had been stopped with its own cotton hood… And with a faded orange hair ribbon its chubby hands had been bound up under its chin." The dead child received a similar treatment, "Across the nose and mouth was a large burdock leaf, over this the child's hood had been tightly drawn, and around and around was bound a quantity of rope yarn. Suffocation must have quickly followed the application of this horrible contrivance…" Despite the hideous circumstances, or perhaps because of them, the *Star* correspondent felt hyperbole justified. "Its wrists and hands are but bone covered with skin; its face, never, perhaps, pretty in health, is drawn and wasted, the staring eyes sunken deep into the skull, while the evidences of decomposition were apparent." In light of the child having been dead for no more than 18 hours, the startling details of a desiccated corpse could only be the product of his imagination, an imagination that knew what its audience wanted.

Coroner Durkin immediately convened an inquiry, and as had been the case for Peter Wheeler, the police magistrate then decided to get into the act. Stipendiary Magistrate Jamieson insisted that a police inquiry follow the coroner's inquest. Of course, a call was put out for the venerable Detective Power of Halifax, and his quarter of a century of investigative experience. The newshounds dug in. Early news reports reaffirm the fact that witnesses frequently spoke to the journalists first, before testifying. During the inquests into the death, on June 28, *The Globe* noted it was not reproducing Elmer E Young's testimony as he "told the same story already published", while Marie Ward's was omitted as "her evidence was practically the same as already told in her story to the newspaper representatives." This bizarre, intimate relationship between various stakeholders in the press and the justice system continued to the very end of Power's career.

The tramp story quickly collapsed and suspicion focused on the children's female guardian, Hope May Young, whether she was their mother or sister, or one's sister and the other's mother, would be disputed. Both inquiries focused on Hope May Young and her landlord, employer and, possibly, lover Kingsley Melanson, as the suspects. At the conclusion of the inquiries the pair were put over for trial in the Supreme Court of Nova Scotia. The trial was scheduled for September, in Clare, Digby County. Two months before then, on Dominion Day, Detective Power announced to all and sundry, through his reliable correspondents, that Hope May Young had confessed to him on the previous day. As *The Herald* put it, "Hope Young's confession made to Detective Power this afternoon created a sensation throughout the county as far as the telephone lines carried." *The Herald*'s correspondent might just as accurately have said 'created a sensation throughout the *country* as far as the *telegraph* carried.'

The young woman told Detective Power that the child simply expired of natural causes while she was bathing her. Fearing that she would be blamed for the death she panicked, carried the child into the woods and made up the story about tramps. She explained that she then took the second child into the woods to corroborate the tramp story. She expected both children to be found, the youngest safely, and the blame to be placed on the unknown vagrants. Following her conversation with Detective Power she repeated the details of their discussion to the crown prosecutor, Harry L Dennison. "I was afraid Kingsley would blame me for the child's death and took her and Elma to the woods to make it appear as if tramps had done the deed," *The Herald* reported she told them.

The observant might have noticed that this is, in fact, not a confession but rather, exculpation. The elder child died a natural death according to the accused. Taking the corpse into the woods might constitute an indignity to a human body, but she had confessed to the child dying a natural death, not her murdering the little one. However, Power and the press were having none of it. As *The Herald* delicately put it: "Her story, however, while not accepted in detail as far as it goes, does not implicate any person other than herself..." Implicitly, the reader can only assume that since no one else did it, she did it. Unasked was the question of whether murder or a natural death ended the child's life. *The Globe* was blunt: "Her story is contradictory and it is believed she is insane." Regardless, before the Supreme Court in September, largely on the basis of the testimony of the esteemed Detective Power, Hope May Young was found guilty of murder in the death of Minnie Alice 'May' Young. Kingsley Melanson was absolved of any involvement in the death, the movement of the body or the attempt to blame tramps. The surviving infant was taken into custody and to Boston by her father, Elmer E Young. Hope May Young was to be hanged on December 20.

The verdict was immediately appealed by her lawyer. The press opined that the best basis for an appeal was a claim that May Young was not fit to stand trial. They were wrong. The appeal focused on two elements of the trial. It disputed the medical evidence originally introduced at the coroner's inquiry that was taken to indicate foul play, specifically strangulation. If that conclusion was not correct, no evidence contradicted May Young's claim that the child died a natural death. However, he did not hit the mark with the majority of the justices until he objected to the admission as evidence of her comments to Detective Power and subsequent statement to Dennison.

He argued that she had been misled by Power and induced to make her statement and if this sounds like a repeat of the Bram case that's because it was. The verdict was overturned and a new trial ordered because her conversation with Power and subsequent statement to Dennison were deemed inadmissible. Her counsel had objected to the interviews and statement at the time describing them "as entirely most unregular and most unfair" to *The Digby Weekly Chronicle*. He raised his objections with Detective Power who dismissed them, saying "they would not be countenanced by any court."

The bad detective was sorely mistaken. The Court of Appeal savaged Power's actions. Justice Graham decided that the accused had been led to believe by Detective Power that he "was acting in her interests", that this constituted an inducement (an inducement predicated on a bald-faced lie) and that the inducement had carried over, in Young's mind, to her subsequent statement to the crown prosecutor. He also noted approvingly that Young's counsel had raised the issue at the time, long before the trial. Justice Russell concurred. According to *The Digby Weekly Chronicle*, he ruled that Young "may have been betrayed into making a statement by supposing it would be favourable to her interest." Further, "nothing was done to remove any impression which the prisoner might have retained from the interview with the detective" when she made her statement to crown prosecutor Dennison.

He concluded that the admission of this tainted evidence rendered a new trial necessary. Power was legally obliged to explain his role as a detective, specifically that anything she said could, and, would be used against her in a court of law. He did not. In fact, he told her the exact opposite. He explicitly said that speaking to him would "probably serve her as well as other ends". Detective Power lied to Hope May Young. Bad detectives lie and see their evidence dismissed. This is precisely what happened in this trial. The prosecution was undermined by Power's bad procedures, namely, another inadmissible confession. The bad detective blew another investigation. He repeated, a decade later, the same mistake he had made while investigating the *Herbert Fuller* murders.

Justice Townshend, the judge who sentenced Peter Wheeler to death, dissented in a unique way. He argued that the evidence was admissible and caught the contradiction. He concluded that the evidence should be admitted and that it absolved Young of murder as the child had died by natural causes. Pause and think about it for a moment. Two justices found Power's interrogation technique underhanded and the evidence inadmissible. The third declared Power's alleged 'confession' to exonerate the accused young mother. No matter how you shake it the great detective went zero for three with the justices of the Nova Scotia Court of Appeal. He also deceived a grief-stricken young mother and put her through the wringer.

Separated by a decade the Young and Bram cases capture a bad detective at his worst. In both instances, with only slight variations, his interrogation techniques were deemed to be unacceptable. Rubbing salt into the great detective's wounds, Mr Justice Graham cited the US Court of Appeal's ruling in the Bram case in disallowing Power's evidence. The great detective's previous failure came back to bite him in the behind. Justifiably so, his aggressive interrogation technique had again ruined an investigation. Not only was Power a bad detective, he was apparently incapable of learning from his mistakes, ensuring he remained a bad detective. Nevertheless, by the time Hope May Young was retried, Detective Power had long passed on to his just reward. Upon the retirement of Chief John O'Sullivan, Power was appointed Chief of the Halifax Police Department, effective January 1, 1906. His time as a detective had finished, while his last murder investigation was still before the courts, amidst a case that encapsulated his career. Once he had fixated on Hope May Young, she was guilty and as good as convicted to his mind. He lied to her to get the statement and it was even a stretch to see the statement as a confession. Regardless, once Power had made up his mind who his prey was, he was relentless.

CHAPTER NINE

The Chief (1906–1907)

THE SLOW economic decline that settled over Nova Scotia in the closing decades of the 19th century was bucked in the northeast of the province, particularly industrialising Pictou County and Cape Breton Island. The economic growth in these two regions was propelled by the original black gold, anthracite. The most valuable variety of coal, it has the fewest impurities and the highest energy density of all coals. In the age of steam, before the internal combustion engine, coal was essential to producing the power that drove engines all over the world.

Cape Breton Island is one mile from northeastern Nova Scotia across the Strait of Canso. Prior to the opening of the Canso Causeway on August 13, 1955 the island was only connected to the mainland by ferry. Coal had been mined on Cape Breton since the early 18th century when the French exploited the resource to provide fuel for Fort Louisbourg. When Cape Breton passed to Great Britain in 1763, coal mining was controlled by royal warrant. Frederick, Duke of York, was granted sole right by the Crown. He subleased the rights to a syndicate of British investors called the General Mining Association. According to the Cape Breton Miners Museum, after this arrangement ended in 1856 and private investment was encouraged, coal mining flourished. "From 1858 to 1893, more than 30 coal mines were opened in the province." In May 1887, Nova Scotian MP Charles Tupper reported to the House of Commons that in 1885, a typical year, Cape Breton mines had produced 1,255,000 tons of coal, representing 95% of Nova Scotia's production and 65% of total Canadian production. The vast coal resources inspired the development of steel mills in the wake of the Second Industrial Revolution.

In 1893, Henry Melville Whitney and Frederick Stark Pearson of Boston, Massachusetts, formed the Dominion Coal Company (DOMCO) with Benjamin Franklin Pearson of the People's Heat and Light Company of Halifax, Nova Scotia. Their operations were concentrated south of Sydney, on the eastern tip of the island. In March 1899 Whitney expanded his operations, establishing the Dominion Iron & Steel Company Ltd. (DISCO). Coming on line in 1901, DISCO's operations on the south side of the Sydney Harbour included coke ovens which cooked coal to create coke to fuel its oxygen blast furnaces that were used to smelt iron ore it extracted at its mine on Bell Island in Newfoundland and shipped to Sydney.

The eponymous small hamlet of Dominion, known by locals as Old Bridgeport, was located north of Sydney on the south shore of Indian Bay, clustered around the pithead of Dominion No 1 coal mine. In the early hours of Friday, February 16, 1906, alongside the Sydney & Louisburg Railroad, south of Dominion, a horrible tragedy occurred. The company house occupied by Austrian immigrant Anton Stetka, his wife and two young daughters, caught fire. Reports as to the fire's discovery varied. Engineer Alexander McKinnon stated he was pulling a string of empty coal cars up to the pithead when he noticed a small, one-storey frame house in flames. Other reports, such as *The Globe,* indicated, "The fire was first seen about 1.40 in the morning by James McAulay, a miner, who was returning from his work at the Reserve mine." The fire may have been noticed by both men simultaneously, they may have been simply locals seeking attention, or, as was often the case, the newspaper may have been wrong.

Regardless of the blaze's discovery, its immediate aftermath was ghastly. Clearing away the smouldering wreckage the charred bodies of the head of the household, his wife, and their two small children were discovered. True to form, *The Herald* offered its readers all the gruesome details. "The head of the father was almost separated from the body. Near the top of the skull was a large hole… There was also an aperture in the skull of the mother and the children's heads were broken on the left side. The father and mother were charred almost beyond recognition, while the children presented the appearance of being cooked." The headline on *The Toronto Daily Star* screamed, "AN ENTIRE FAMILY CRUELLY MURDERED" over a lead that concluded, "Skulls of Parents Crushed in with Axe". While the article itself was short, it concluded definitively, "The theory receiving most credence is that the whole family was murdered by an enemy."

The Globe (Toronto) noted, "The skulls of all were crushed in and an axe was found between the beds on which the parents and children were sleeping." Then *The Globe* went further, concurring with the *Star*, "although the building was only partially burned, those who gathered about the house found it impossible to arouse the inmates, a fact which tends to the belief that the house was set on fire to conceal the murder… The foulest murder ever known in Nova Scotia." *The Globe*'s coverage guaranteed that readers would stay tuned, "There is much yet to be revealed perhaps, more than will ever come out. The horror of it all sinks into the hearts of the people, and no effort will be spared to place the blame where it belongs." The murder of a family of four, and the attempt to hide the crime by torching the house and immolating the corpses immediately made national headlines.

There seemed to be three possible narratives. The fire, through smoke inhalation or immolation, had accidentally killed the family. They had been murdered and the fire started to hide the crime, possibly, initially, a robbery. Finally, Anton Stetka had, for reasons unknown, murdered his wife and children, set the fire, and then taken his own life. Placing the blame where it belonged would prove no easy task.

Typical of the time, two things happened immediately. Coroner Phelan empanelled a jury and started an inquiry. At the same time, due to the gravity of the crime, an appeal was made, through the provincial Attorney General, for the services of Detective Nicholas Power. In fact, as of New Year's Day, he was Chief Power. Nonetheless, although tardy, he would arrive a week after the murder, following the release of the coroner's report on the deaths.

The coroner's inquest convened at 10 o'clock on the morning of the fire in the Sydney Provincial Workmen's Association hall, also doubling as a temporary morgue. Multiple witnesses testified the Stetkas "were known to be good people and bore excellent characters", according to *The Herald*. Drs Murphy and Morrison testified that they could not confirm the cause of death as all four bodies were too badly burned. It could have been smoke inhalation, incineration, blows from a blunt instrument such as the axe found at the scene, or physical damage wrought as the house collapsed onto the victims. Dr

Morrison noted that the parents' bodies were far more burned than the children and suggested they may have been soaked in a flammable liquid before the fire was started. This, of course, implied that all four were dead before the fire started and not killed by the fire. Satisfied that the bodies would offer no useful clues, all four were interred that afternoon, a mere 12 hours after the crime.

In an effort to resolve the situation, the children's bodies were later exhumed and the doctors were ordered to perform an autopsy and ascertain cause of death. Again, they delivered incomplete conclusions. While stating explicitly there was no clear evidence of murder, they did not rule it out. Limply they suggested that "the cracks in the skull may have been caused with contact with a hot wire, say with a wire mattress, and they expressed the opinion that the inmates were suffocated." By suffocated they mean smoke inhalation, not murder by strangulation or asphyxiation, such as a pillow pressed over the face. That a 'hot wire' could have caused the children's skulls to explode is tenuous at best.

On Saturday, witness T J Brady, a neighbour, identified the axe as one he kept in his woodshed that was no longer there. Ivan Kempe and Alex McKinnon were the first on the scene. The latter stated that "the clothes on the bed were not on fire yet" and Kempe testified, "the smoke poured out very thickly from the kitchen window." Next, Mrs Morgan, who lived two doors away from the Stetkas, was called "but expressed ignorance of almost everything that had transpired." The fire had apparently started in the kitchen, at the back of the house while the bodies were all in the bedroom at the front of the house, this much was clear. However, with the cause of death unknown, an important question remained unanswered: had the victims died of smoke inhalation or were they already dead when the fire started? The latter was murder, the former a tragic accident. The inquiry heard from more than 30 witnesses, over six days. However, the evidence had done little to clarify the timeline—namely, death as a result of the fire or prior to it. With this question unanswered it was impossible to determine whether murder had occurred or it was a case of death by misadventure.

Coroner Phelan delivered the jury's verdict at 4.30pm on Thursday, February 22. Not surprisingly, the jury delivered an open verdict. They acknowledged that they could not confidently assign a cause and manner of death:

> In connection with the death of Anton Stetka, of his wife and his two children, which occurred at Old Bridgeport, in the county of Cape Breton, on or about February 16, 1906 we desire to state that after having all the evidence produced and weighing the same most carefully, we believe that the said deaths occurred under most unusual and suspicious circumstances, and would recommend further inquiry under the direct supervision of the Crown.

Two elements of the statement merit note. They did not rule out murder (nor had the children's autopsies), but they did describe the four deaths as "unusual and suspicious", in layman's terms, "it might have been murder". *The Globe* turned suspicion into fact: "The inquiry was very careful and exhaustive, and exploded the accident and suicide theories completely, but has not located the murderers." *The Globe* managed to make two mistakes in this short sentence. First, recalling Peter Wheeler's railroading, a coroner's inquest was not supposed to 'locate the murderers' or identify suspects. Coroner Lovett's unjustified decision to do so set Peter Wheeler on the road to his death. Moreover, the inquest had not dismissed the accident or suicide explanations and settled on murder as the cause of death. It had done the very opposite. It had not ruled out any potential causes of death, describing events as "most unusual and suspicious". These errors and transformation of an open verdict into one of murder, are typical of the era of yellow journalism.

However, to be fair, this interpretation, that the jury suspected murder, is given added weight by their recommendation that 'further inquiry under the direct supervision of the Crown' be undertaken. An open verdict meant the jury was vexed. It did not necessarily consider the deaths to be murder, but it did not rule out murder. It meant the jury felt more qualified and experienced investigators should undertake a second investigation into the deaths. In these circumstances it was almost inevitable that the Crown's investigation would be undertaken by the recently promoted chief of the Halifax Police Department, Nicholas Power.

On February 16 *The Globe*'s correspondent had breathlessly described his visit to the scene: "Only a wall and about two feet of the chimney remained of the house. The cellar was filled with ashes and twisted kitchen utensils, and an axe lay between where the two beds had been." He was far from the only visitor. By the time of Power's arrival, almost a week after the fire, the crime scene had been contaminated by countless visitors. Clearly, the crime scene offered little meaningful to Power. This meant that he had no physical evidence to go on, only the evidence already presented at the inquiry. The coroner's inquest had concluded inconclusively but this did not prevent Power from quickly reaching a definitive answer and, true to fashion, rushing to announce it to the newsmen.

On Monday, February 26 *The Glace Bay Gazette* reported Detective Power had reached his verdict. Anticipating a future, more media-savvy age, Power presented the interviewer with a series of well-planned talking points. Unusually, they are actually numbered in the newspaper copy. "1st. I am here at the request of the attorney-general." Next, he concurred with the coroner's inquiry that this tragedy was "a very mysterious and serious matter" (befitting, the talents of Canada's Sherlock Holmes, seems implicit). "3rd. The doctors' report says that other than burning they fail to find the cause of death (implying, without justification, that 'burning' was the cause of death). The jury and doctors in my opinion are quite correct."

His fourth and final point is a masterful example of solipsistic bafflegab. Slipping two points into one he asserts that he is a renowned expert with a reputation for being right: "I have had some experience in investigating suspicious fires and their causes, and I have more than once come to a correct solution on the conclusion of matters of that kind." Following this self-endorsement, he grandly concludes, "I have arrived at the conclusion that no crime was committed. My belief is that the Stetka family were asleep, when the fire, in some mysterious way, occurred near the front door of the house..." This assertion directly contradicts the inquest's conclusion that the cause of death was undetermined and multiple eyewitnesses who testified to the fire starting in the back of the house. Power, unlike the open verdict of the coroner's inquest he claims to agree with, arrived "at the conclusion that no crime was committed", implying their deaths were caused by the fire.

This definitive conclusion could not have been based on any new physical evidence. If Power even visited the crime scene, it was days after the fire, the crime scene was disturbed and contaminated, and the bodies were already in the ground. In a nutshell, there was no evidence left, nothing to investigate. There is also no evidence that Power read transcripts of the inquiry's evidence or consulted the coroner. But a bad detective does not need evidence. The 'Man who saved the Prince' had his reputation to stand on and so his lecture began with the assertion, "I have more than once come to a correct solution on the conclusion of matters of that kind." Power's only evidence is his reputation (and his ego).

And that was that. On Monday, February 26, ten days after the deaths of an entire family, including a four-year-old boy and an infant girl, Power shut down any further investigation despite the physical evidence and presence of a murder weapon. He did so on the authority of his reputation, largely fallacious, not the evidence in the case. He did not engage in detection, he simply pulled rank. The 'Man who saved the Prince', with 25 years' experience, and now the chief of the largest police department in the Maritimes, was issuing a pronouncement from on high, one not to be questioned, and it amounted to 'move along folks, nothing to see here'.

Expressing gratitude for small mercies, and knowing Power's history, one must appreciate that he did not accuse an innocent of the crime as he had many times in the past. Nor did he conduct interviews that were illegal, as he had in the cases of Thomas Bram and May Hope Young. These grievous life-destroying errors do not play a part in the case. However, as had been the situation with Thomas Bram, if the Stetkas were murdered, Power's peremptory conclusions meant that a multiple murderer went free. Further, this was not a case of 'murdered by persons unknown'. There was a huge backstory to the Stetka murders that Power must have been aware of and chose to ignore. This was par for the course for Power at this stage in his career. Justice was an intangible, actual detective work was demanding and often inconclusive, but media attention tending towards sycophancy was real, and a balm to the bad detective's ego. Why bother to investigate when one can pontificate?

The Stetkas were hardly anonymous, faceless immigrants, they were caught up in a complex and violent community melodrama that offered motive aplenty and a clear suspect. It was a community quarrel more complex than Game of Thrones. Power simply swept this avenue of investigation under the rug.

In February 1906 the immigrant dream had faded for the Stetkas and they were preparing to return to Austria. A mine manager told the coroner's inquest that Mrs Stetka had given notice on their company house and requested a cash refund on their deposit that he had promised to have ready the next day. Other witnesses testified that the Stetkas' belongings were packed in preparation for departure. While economics may have played a role in their decision, it is plain that they were on the outside in a community dispute. Mrs Morgan, who lived two doors away from the Stetkas, and 'expressed ignorance of almost everything that had transpired' was telling a bald-faced lie. She had intimate knowledge of, and involvement in, the sordid affair.

Mrs Morgan ran a boarding house and the residents included some of her children, including her adult son James Snelgrove. Originally from Newfoundland, the family and boarding house had something of a reputation and its residents were not unfamiliar with the criminal justice system. In fact, only hours after the fire, that very morning, James Snelgrove was scheduled to go to trial, charged with rape (the name of the criminal offence at the time). The victim was none other than Mrs Stetka. It was alleged that he sexually assaulted her while Anton was away at work. The evidence must have been overwhelming. Despite the death of the victim (needless to add, she did not testify) he was convicted and sentenced to four years in Dorchester Penitentiary. Mysteriously dying only hours before she was to testify against James Snelgrove is a decidedly "suspicious circumstance". Snelgrove had motive, living only a short distance away he had opportunity, and it is reasonable to assume he would have known a neighbour, Brady, left his woodshed unlocked and an axe at hand. All of this was ignored by Power.

Equally overwhelming was the byzantine manoeuvring behind the scenes. It was rumoured that the victim, encouraged by her axe-owning neighbour, T J Brady, had contrived to make the allegation only to force James Snelgrove to offer a cash settlement of $500 from a recent windfall. Counter allegations held that Mrs Morgan, Snelgrove's mother, had offered a cash bounty to Mrs Stetka if she would withdraw the charges or not testify.

She also suggested James's behaviour should be excused as he was drunk and acting out of character. Clearly, Mrs Morgan knew more than she had told the coroner's inquest. So did the press. The *St John Daily Sun* put it plainly, "The attempt at rape by Snelgrove in the absence of Mr Stetka caused much talk, and the Stetkas felt the position keenly, and said they were going back to Austria where they formerly belonged." It is powerfully hard to believe that a media maven like Power was unaware of the newspaper reports of a veritable Peyton Place.

This is not to convict James Snelgrove of murder, as well as rape. It is not necessary to convict Snelgrove to indict Power. Power, initially, had to decide whether or not an investigation was merited, not to decide whether or not James Snelgrove committed the murders. Power's situation was akin to that of the coroner. The coroner's ambit was limited to the manner of death only. Power's initial responsibility was limited to determining if the law may have been broken and further investigation was justified. He was not obliged to identify a suspect or even decide if the deaths were murders. He only needed to acknowledge further investigation was merited. He did not. Power decided to pull the plug on any further investigation. To do so he had to ignore the context, the criminal proceedings and the links between the Stetkas and Snelgrove/Morgan. He could not have been unaware of the situation as it fuelled the rumour mill and filled the newspapers. For Nic Power to declare categorically that the deaths were accidental and did not merit further investigation he had to willfully ignore the complex backstory to the Stetkas' deaths. Assuming the deaths were murder, probably by James Snelgrove or his agents, as was the case with wrongfully convicted Peter Wheeler, somewhere a multiple murderer or murderers were living unpunished.

This is Nic Power at his worst. A detective shutting down scrutiny: an investigative oxymoron. What happened and what was going on at the time cannot be clearly discerned today. It is plain, however, there was more than meets the eye behind the story. This ambiguity alone, let alone coupled with the open verdict, demanded 'further inquiry'. That there was no investigation is directly attributable to Power's pomposity. With no evidence and no explanation other than the self-serving assertion 'I have had some experience in investigating suspicious fire and their causes, and I have more than once come to a correct solution on the conclusion of matters of that kind' he closed the door on resolving the mystery surrounding the death of the Stetka family. When Power ruled the deaths accidental and short-circuited any investigation, he made an early report in *The Globe* seem prescient. "There is much yet to be revealed perhaps, more than will ever come out." One thing that will never come out is the identity of the person or persons who murdered the entire Stetka family.

Motive remains unfathomable, but it is undeniable that

Chief Power shut down any investigation. Perhaps he was unsatisfied with his lodging. Perhaps he was unhappy with the dreary, grey backwater of Sydney, isolated on Cape Breton Island. Perhaps he yearned for his new, spacious office and the attendant privileges and responsibilities that came with being chief. But probably he was in a hurry to get back to Halifax because he was facing a storm of criticism. This was the newly promoted chief's first egregious decision. It would not be his last. As chief, however, his greatest sins would lie in different fields. The bad detective would prove an equally bad chief.

Nicholas Power was promoted to chief of the Halifax Police Department, effective January 1, 1906. Unlike the conflict that had characterised the selection of John Sullivan a dozen years earlier, Power acceded to the position with no other candidates and little discussion at the committee and council level. He immediately ran into a significant problem before he found himself called to Cape Breton Island.

Unsurprisingly, newspaper hysteria and headlines accompanied the beheading of widowed farmer Freeman Harvie, near Ellershouse in Hants County, 35 miles north west of Halifax. On Wednesday, February 7, 1906, under the lead "Finding of the Saw That Severed Harvie's Head", *The Herald* reported graphically, "It is an ordinary hand saw, only about half of which remains and while the blood had been largely wiped from the iron the wooden handle is stained with red." The old man's headless corpse was found at the foot of the cellar stairs of his isolated farmhouse.

George Stanley (aka John Ryan, John Cavanaugh and M Byrne) was quickly arrested for the crime and rightly so. He was plainly guilty. He confessed to being a party to the killing but not the murderer. The old man was looking to sell his farm and remove himself from Ellershouse. Stanley deceitfully expressed an interest in purchasing it. He planned to kill Harvie, eliminating the need to pay him, dispose of the body and explain to neighbours that Harvie had left the district after being paid for the farm. The problem for Power was not one of detection, as he was not involved in the investigation. It was one of incarceration. Power's department should have had Harvie under arrest and in jail before he fled Halifax. As *The Herald* put it: "The police were lax."

Stanley had only arrived in Halifax from Ireland on December 20, 1905 aboard the *Siberian*. It was later determined that he had escaped from an Irish prison and was fleeing the country. Aboard ship he made the acquaintance of Thomas P Forsey, who invited Stanley to lodge at his boarding house located on Smith Street at the south end of Barrington Street. Stanley stayed a little over three weeks. On Saturday morning, January 13, he disappeared and headed north to a hotel in Bedford, registering under an alias. On Tuesday, skipping out on his bill, he continued north, landing in Hants County where he murdered Harvie.

Stanley fled Halifax because he had fleeced his landlord and fellow boarders. His landlord's wife discovered $45 missing when she opened her money box to pay a bill. A boarder lost $40 when he discovered his trunk had been broken into. Subsequent to Stanley's flight, Mrs Forsey also discovered jewellery and Mexican coins missing.

In a unique illustration of how intimately newspapers involved themselves in investigations, the Mexican coins eventually turned up, in the pocket of a *Herald* correspondent. In Hants County, Stanley had given the coin to another man for reasons unclear, perhaps a purchase or repayment of a debt. That man, Dave Fischer, was subsequently picked up, interrogated, searched and found to have a quarter on his person. *The Herald* assured its readers that it had been earned legally as it was the very quarter their reporter had paid Fischer for the Mexican coin he had received from Stanley. In the midst of an active murder investigation *The Herald* did not hesitate to purchase evidence and proudly announced it had done so. The legal ruckus that would follow from such practices today can only be imagined.

Power's problem was one of timing. On the evening of Friday, January 12, boarder S A Fulton and landlord Thomas Forsey had walked up Barrington Street from the boarding house to city hall, entered the basement police station, waited for Chief Power to return from dinner and, upon his return at eight o'clock, placed a complaint against

Stanley for the theft of $40. Then, nothing happened. It was after 10 o'clock the next morning before a constable arrived at the Smith Street boarding house and by then Stanley had flown the coop for Bedford and beyond, footloose and fancy free to defraud and decapitate old Freeman Harvie. A lead in *The Herald* lamented: "Had he been arrested Harvie would be alive today." The complaint was placed directly with Power. Fulton, a mere boarder and possibly transient, had his complaint corroborated by his landlord, a local property owner. There was no excuse for Power's failure to act and no one else was to blame. Power had not acted and a murder resulted.

The next day Chief Power responded to the accusations of laxity by dismissing them out of hand. He told *The Herald* that despite his genius and long success as a detective he would never be a 'mind-reader'. He could not have known that Stanley would flee, nor that he was capable of murder. Power did not offer an explanation, and heaven forbid an apology. He dismissed the criticism as naive optimism, a demand for foresight that no human being could possess. In the pages of *The Herald* Fulton responded, speaking truth to Power, with vigour, "Promptness in action and not 'mind-reading' ability was all that was required to have given the Halifax police the credit for locking up a bold thief who afterwards, no doubt, committed one of the worst murders in the annals of Nova Scotia."

A week later, when he was called to Cape Breton to

deal with the Stetka murders, he was in the midst of a media storm and in the uncomfortable and unfamiliar role of media miscreant, not media darling. Fortunately for Nic, as is its want, the pack of baying newshounds soon moved on to new stories. The Stetka murders was one of those stories and the other was the largest fire in the history of Moncton, New Brunswick. On February 24, a fire, starting in the paint shop, destroyed the Intercolonial Railway works causing over $1,000,000 damage and threatening the entire downtown before it was extinguished. The brouhaha over the Harvie affair slowly dissipated. Nothing will change the fact that Power did not act with alacrity. Had he done so, Stanley would have been cooling his heels in Halifax City Hall's basement cells, not beheading Freeman Harvie. Power did not cause Harvie's death, but he could have prevented it. For a bloodhound, proud of his man-hunting successes, George Stanley was the one who got away, with fatal consequences.

Two months into the top job, the bad detective was failing miserably as a chief. The press was up in arms about the Harvie murder, a very public and unfamiliar affront to the 'Man who saved the Prince'. On the down low and unknown at the time, he had let the murderer or murderers of an entire family escape justice. It was hardly an auspicious start.

Chief Power attempted to reset the narrative as spring arrived. His most noteworthy achievement in that role, typically, had nothing to do with improving the department and everything to do with improving the department's image. His image-savvy response is a corollary to the intense discomfort he must have felt seeing the press criticise his handling of the Stanley incident. Acknowledging Power's awareness of, and attention to, his own image, this is hardly surprising. Power's self-proclaimed greatest achievement as chief was the re-accoutrement of his troops. His lasting legacy was to be sartorial splendour, a sterling example of his lifelong belief that image outweighed reality. His quidditative response to every problem was to make things *look* better.

Power's personal problem was bad press over the Harvie affair. The problems for his department as a whole, apparently timeless, were ongoing complaints before the Police Committee against members of the force for drunkenness or from the public for illegal search, overbearing behaviour and excessive violence. Power's solution was simple, and simply fantastic. If the police were better attired, they would receive greater respect from the public and the citizenry would be less likely to complain. To Power's mind the problem was not the performance of his department, it was lack of respect among the public. And perfectly logical, to the paths his mind wandered, improved appearance would enhance their public image, ergo, complaints would decrease. His solution did not address the problem, it merely dressed up the problem.

Nonetheless, he proudly announced this programme to *The Herald* amid the patriotic, Imperial hoopla surrounding Victoria Day. Power proudly told the correspondent that his aim was "to make his men among the best dressed in [North] America." Testifying to the weight of his reputation at this point in his career, he persuaded a parsimonious police committee and council to support his initiative at considerable expense as annual uniform costs skyrocketed with the capital expense of two sets (summer and winter) of new uniforms for the entire department, including everything from belts to outerwear and everything in-between: "Another innovation that is being introduced is that the men will wear uniform collars. The "Dewey" and ties of uniform colours, black," *The Herald* reported. When it came to the appearance of his men, Power was willing to spare no expense.

His second innovation was incorporated into the new uniforms. Police personnel wore coloured service badges spiraling up their uniform sleeves indicating their years of service and level of experience. For every five years of service a constable received an additional light blue service badge. Power reasoned that this too would reduce citizen complaints. If an officer with a single service badge indicating he was a novice made an error, a citizen would attribute it to inexperience and indulge the beginner rather than complain.

If a possessor of many service badges indicating experience did something not strictly by the book, a responsible citizen would assume that the officer knew best on the basis of his long experience and, again, not complain.

Chief Power, with 41 years' service would, alone, wear a gaggle of eight service badges up his sleeve, the most of any man serving. The day after Victoria Day, 1906, Chief Power explained the new system's benefits to a *Herald* newsman, "It will save the men from a lot of unjust criticism" and encourage the public to treat veterans with "consideration and respect". The occasion for the coverage was the first public parade of the men in their new summer uniforms, scheduled for 2pm the following day.

True to form, Power was focused on improving the appearance, not the performance, of his charges. The entire exercise was directed to improving their image to reduce complaints, not to improving performance to reduce complaints. Nic Power had a one-track mind, and like Potemkin, he placed infinitely more importance on image than reality, on appearance rather than performance. When he assumed the senior role in the department, he reimagined his personnel as the best dressed on the continent. To him that was a significant achievement, one of greater importance than the arrest of the Stetkas' murderers or Freeman Harvie's life.

Nic Power's tenure as chief culminated in his outrageous and very public resignation after less than two years at the top of the department. He arranged to have his letter of resignation published in both *The Herald* and *The Chronicle*, and in it he laid on the Irish charm. He described the decision as a "painful moment" but acknowledged that "young and ambitious men on the force" sensing the prospect of advancement would work with "increased interest, energy and zeal" and he owed them that opportunity. He then thanked all and sundry, the police commissioners, His Worship Mayor MacIlreith, the deputy mayor, various aldermen, the bureaucracy, his fellow lawmen and Haligonians at large, humbly concluding, "Trusting that this may meet with your approval, I remain, very respectfully yours."

It is evident that Power put considerable thought into his resignation letter. It is well written and organised. Given the preceding précis one might wonder what Power was requesting approval of in the above valediction. He was requesting approval of a claim he made in the very first paragraph of his letter. Before the social niceties, Chief Power opened his letter with a demand. Its position as the lead speaks to how important it was to Power. Its enormity speaks to his inflated sense of self-worth and entitlement. "I would ask you allow me on retiring the same superannuation [pension] as that given to my predecessor, Mr John O'Sullivan, which I am advised you can do under the authority of an Act of the Legislature passed last year." The bottom line, his bottom line, was the first order of business. As to the demand itself, Power was demanding the same pension as his predecessor. On its surface it was not unreasonable. However, Power served as chief less than two years, 23 months to be precise.

In contrast, Chief O'Sullivan had held the position

for more than a dozen years, from the 1892 reorganisation until December 31, 1905. Power was demanding the same pension as a man who had held the position for almost seven times as long as he had. It was granted. The missive is a perfect cap to Power's career. The most important point, in his mind, was his pension and to his mind, he was entitled to that which his predecessor had received, despite his brief tenure. To Nic Power, Nic Power came first; before the police department and any other temporal, lower-case powers, and certainly before abstract concepts like truth and justice. His overwhelming sense of entitlement and his grandiose sense of self-worth are captured in a resignation letter in which the first order of business is an outrageously exorbitant and undeserved financial demand. For the bad detective Nic Power always came first.

Focused on his public persona as Canada's Sherlock Holmes and positive newspaper coverage of his infallibility, Nic Power was a bad detective who was frequently wrong. As chief he vehemently denied responsibility for a deadly error, terminated an investigation into four very suspicious deaths and repeated his misplaced emphasis on appearances, mistaking tailoring prestidigitation for reform. The bad detective made a bad chief.

CHAPTER 10

Conclusion

On Halifax Police Department Chief Nicholas Power's retirement, *The Morning Herald* referenced his "long record of criminal 'round-ups'… [suggested], so numerous are those episodes, and so full of interest, it would take a volume to justly recount them." This is that volume. It has demonstrated Power's 'round-ups' were both numerous and of interest. He was, as an unnamed 'well-known citizen' described him, "a strong personality".

The Sherlock Holmes metaphor is absent from this memorial. Power's fantastic deeds are compared to the stirring adventures of the heroes of *Boys Own Annuals*, "real thrilling episodes which would cheer the heart of the hero-worshipping youth, who devours 'Old Sleuth' and 'Nick Carter' with avidity." The 'Old Sleuth' was a detective, unnamed like Hammett's 'Continental Op', created by Harlan Halsey in 1872. He became so popular he was featured in his own monthly publication, *Old Sleuth Library* and, like the 'Yellow Kid', inspired imitators and copyright lawsuits between publishers. While Nick Carter hit the heights of his fame during the Great Depression, the detective made his first appearance in 1886.

On his retirement, Nicholas Power was accorded accolades reserved for fictional heroes. He was Canada's Sherlock Holmes, and hero-worshipping youths' 'Old Sleuth'. Nearing its finale, the praise reaches a crescendo: "His name will ever be enshrined, and it will need no effort to keep his memory green." Unfortunately, the feature, filling a full page and illustrated, loses touch with the reality of Power's spotted career, when it identifies the character traits, the values that make Power a hero and deserving of emulation—"a life of even living, integrity and honesty." Publicly, through the newspapers, Power was portrayed as a great detective retiring at the peak of an illustrious career that spanned almost 50 years.

'Even living' can certainly be conceded: He was never before the department's overseers alleged to have been drunk on duty, a rare distinction for Halifax's men in blue. The only time he was charged with the use of excessive force, during the warranted removal of an infant from its guardian, multiple witnesses testified to the falsity of the quickly dismissed accusation. His domestic life seems to have been unremarkable. Both his marriages ended only with the death of his spouse, and as a widower he lived with a daughter and her family. By all indications our bad detective was a man of moderate and temperate habits, who lived life on an even keel.

In terms of cash register honesty his rectitude seems evident. The sole occasion when an issue of this nature arose was not a question of misappropriation, but rather one of jurisdiction, authority and autonomy. The problem that led to Detective Power's brief suspension in the summer of 1889 did not involve accusations of Power having pocketed the $35 in question. Power's honesty, in terms of dollars and cents, was never questioned. The issue was the detective's unwillingness to provide the names of the parties to whom he had made the payments. It was a question of how much authority the Police Committee had over the department's detective, and how much autonomy Detective Power was entitled to, not larceny. Detective Power's prey would have called him a 'square John', a model of middle-class rectitude and moderation.

One is tempted to suggest that he tended toward self-righteousness. This impression is, perhaps, given credence by the only occasion he came out of retirement. In December 1909 *The Globe* reported, "Detective Power has a force of constables on the scene." Specifically, Power was back in Cape Breton, leading a crew of strike-breaking plain clothes men escorting scabs through a United Mine Workers picket line during a drawn out, violent and bloody labour struggle in the coal fields.

Along with nuts and bolts honesty, Power was also a model of late-Victorian manhood in other senses. He personified Victorian manhood as it was expressed at the Halifax Police Department's inception. He was "sober, intelligent, trustworthy, orderly and athletic", all qualities enumerated in the original job qualifications. Setting aside 'trustworthy' for a moment, Nic Power was a model of the desired characteristics of a Halifax guardian, and more broadly a late-Victorian man. Tall, broad and bearded he looked the part. He was evidently willing and able to use his size, scrapping when the circumstances called for it. His naval experience, however brief and inconsequential, reinforced his badge of authority. His staid personal life testifies to his orderliness. His career trajectory, and skill at manipulating the newspapermen speak to his intelligence. Power was a man's man, even among the breed of manly men. And it was a role the 'Man who saved the Prince' loved to play for the press and the public.

However, there were twisted truths at the heart of the Victorian concept of manhood that speaks volumes of Power. This idea of hyper-virile manhood found expression in broader and deeper cultural themes. While Power was guarding the social order in Halifax, imperial explorers were extending that social order geographically. Think of Franklin in the Canadian Arctic, Livingstone in Africa and the subsequent searches for both; the latter concluded successfully by Henry Morton Stanley, whose expedition was funded by *The New York Herald* seeking a scoop. Exploration, like detection, was front page news. With exploration came northern European civilization, specifically Christianity. David Livingstone considered himself a medical missionary, offering both the physical and spiritual benefits of civilization. Underpinning it all was a certain chauvinism—what's on offer is the best on the planet and you need it whether you want it or not.

Interestingly, theologians, even those trapped behind desks rather than safariing across Africa, got in on the act. Church historians refer to the emergence of hyper-virile 'muscular Christianity'. The doctrine held that a faithful Christian man was healthy, athletic and physically dominant because he treated his body like God's temple with proper diet and exercise. Mentally and morally he was superior because of a related sense of duty and discipline. Suffice to say the entire trend is encapsulated in one organisation, the *Salvation Army*, founded in 1878. In a nutshell, to descend to aphorism, might was right because right was might. This was the white man's burden, the responsibility to extend his superior social and moral order to those still labouring under a veil of ignorance. Again, it was all contingent on the chauvinistic belief that what was on offer was the best, in the best of all possible worlds.

Nicholas Power was that world and that chauvinism in microcosm. Coupled with his massive ego, that made him both a very popular and a very bad detective. He was more concerned with his narrative being proven right than convicting the guilty. He was more concerned with the appearance of his success than truth and justice. Consequently, he picked low-hanging fruit. Outsiders, whether they were Fenians or visible minorities, were easy prey.

In one of the earliest occasional papers that he wrote for the Atlantic Institute of Criminology, Peter McGahan refers to Power's storied investigations as 'exploits'. Little did he realise the truth of the term, in multiple senses. Etymologically, exploit's roots lie in two Latin words, *ex* meaning un or out and *plicare* meaning fold. Thus, to exploit something is to unfold it (the relationship is more evident in the word, explicate, derived from the same sources). To investigate a crime is to unfold the circumstances of the act. The detective unfolds the clues and organises them into a plausible narrative that identifies and implicates the perpetrator. As the great, and entirely fictional famous detective Sherlock Holmes put it: "When you have eliminated the impossible, whatever remains, however improbable, must be the truth." Holmes and Power both unfolded mysterious crimes and their adventures were quidditative exploits.

However, exploit has a more aggressive meaning also. A subset of this aggressiveness was amply present in Power. Unfairly taking advantage of another's vulnerabilities is often referred to as 'exploiting a weakness'. Power knew how to exploit the media's weakness. Practically, he realised the importance of newspapers and knew how to manipulate journalists. In contemporary parlance he was a media operative who knew how to handle emerging technology, namely, as primitive as it seems today, newspapers. This coupled with a field of endeavour, investigating murder and mayhem, that obsessed and titillated the newly literate public, assured Power a huge public persona and an international reputation. Detective Nicholas Power succeeded admirably in exploiting journalists to inflate his public image. He used this podium to try cases before the criminal justice system did to push the judge and jury to adopt his narrative. Detective Power exploited the newshounds.

In a subtler, sinister sense, he also exploited the reading public the newspapers delivered his narratives to. He knew their weaknesses, he read their minds better than he read criminals' minds. He brought home prey that his enthralled fans were inclined to see as guilty. Peter Wheeler is the most tragic and obvious illustration of this. Irrefutable medical evidence, available only days after the crime with Dr Ellison's testimony at the coroner's inquest, exculpated Peter Wheeler. It was a physical impossibility for him to have committed the murder because he had multiple witnesses to his presence at his boarding house during the early morning hours Dr Ellison set as the time of death. But he was an easy target and Power was an opportunist. Peter Wheeler was an outsider, a relative newcomer of indeterminate origin.

In a similar fashion, in the same year, Power presumed Bram's guilt from the get-go, to such an extent that he told Bram he was guilty before he interrogated him, meanwhile, working to ensure blue-blooded Lester Monks was not implicated. He also refused to believe that the murderer was a blonde-haired, blue-eyed Swede (despite his previously having attacked a man with a weapon while suffering from paranoid delusions). Like any predator, Power was an opportunist. Bram's ethnicity made him a target for Power and for Power's fans, as did Peter Wheeler's. Whether Power was a racist, or merely pandering to popular sentiment, is a moot point. What is clear is that both Bram and Wheeler had their lives ruined (and in one case ended) by Power's almost instantaneous assertions that they were the culprits, long before he had done any actual detective work.

Despite the minor dynamite smuggling charges that Breckton and Holmes were eventually convicted of, the case counts as the most significant in understanding Power's policing career and the man, the bad detective, himself. Conveniently, it was his first major case following his promotion to the rank of detective. In simple, chronological terms it was the foundation of his reputation, he would be forever known as the 'Man who saved the Prince'. Second, his supposed unravelling of this non-existent plot remained true in the public mind, so true that it became his foundation myth—both justification for, and evidence of, his monumental detection skills. Detective Nic Power could foresee future events. He could take seemingly unconnected pieces of evidence, overlooked or dismissed by others and construct a chain of evidence that revealed crimes and their perpetrators. The popular belief that he possessed these skills made him Canada's Sherlock Holmes.

The problem, of course, is that Detective Power had done nothing of the kind. He had created a conspiracy out of whole cloth. There was, in fact, nothing there. Poor Holmes and Breckton whiled away a year of their lives in Rockwood Prison because Nic Power was full of himself, and the press and public lapped it up. Foundation myth as it became, and remains in many circles, it reveals Power's sleazy *modus operandi*. Upon arrest of his culprit (victim?) Power would immediately rush to the press and have them broadcast his narrative widely and sensationally. He would then obstinately stick to that story, using his reputation as the 'Man who saved the Prince' to give it credence.

The final word belongs to another Irishman, G B Shaw. In a slight but hilarious one-act play entitled 'How He Lied to Her Husband', 'he' tries to persuade 'she' to leave 'the husband' while the pair await his return. 'She' desperately attempts to cool his ardour and have him deny the affair to 'the husband'. Conceding to her wishes, 'he' surrenders. "Very well. You have broken my spirit and desecrated my dreams. I will lie and protest and stand on my honor: oh, I will play the gentleman, never fear... I'm capable of anything now. I should not have told him the truth by halves; and now I will not lie by halves. I'll wallow in the honor of a gentleman."

Self-confident and full of himself, bearish and brash, Nic Power was a model of a Victorian detective straight from central casting. Incredibly egotistical, he conflated his image with honour, and appealed to popular sentiment with justice. The fact of the matter is you could trust Nic Power with two bits, but you could not trust him with your life. He had no integrity and his loyalty was to only himself and his image. This made him a very bad detective. Twice, in the Young and Bram cases, convictions were overturned due to his aggressive, duplicitous interrogations. His rush to judgement and brash public statements led to the lynching of Peter Wheeler and shut down an investigation into the savage murder of the entire Stetka family. His nonchalance as chief led to Freeman Harvie's beheading. The bad detective's track record was terrible, yet with extraordinary media savvy he managed to bury it under the lie that he was the 'Man who Saved the Prince'.

Was it hubris? Did he become convinced of his infallibility? Was he desperate to maintain his media persona? Was he desperate to maintain his infallibility and persona in his own mind? Perhaps he suffered from pareidolia, the tendency to see a specific pattern or meaningful images in random stimuli. Some secrets will never be revealed and the full definitive history of Detective Nicholas Power will never be written. The bad detective's twisted inner thoughts can never be known, but the lives he ruined testify to a bad detective who wallowed in his honour.